Companies
For Good

LIVING WITH MODERN CAPITALISM

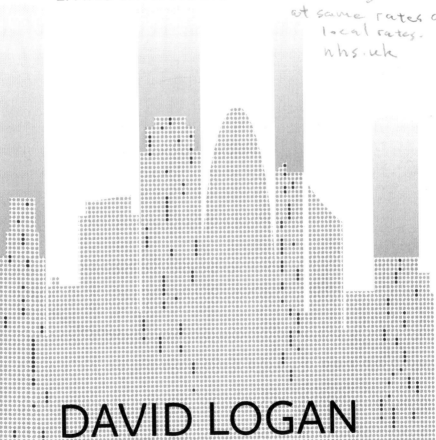

DAVID LOGAN

Companies For Good

First published in 2021 by

Panoma Press Ltd
48 St Vincent Drive, St Albans, Herts, AL1 5SJ, UK
info@panomapress.com
www.panomapress.com

Book layout by Neil Coe.

978-1-784529-35-2

To, Anupama, a fellow traveller on this difficult road !! Love.

Dedication

This book is dedicated to Mary Bayliss who inspired me as a teenager with her teaching of economic history, and also her husband Fred, an adult educator and senior civil servant; they were both lifelong, and supportive friends to me.

Testimonials

"With boots-on-the-ground worldwide experience David Logan is a pioneer once again asking great questions about the role of business in creating our common future. A must read."

Dr. Jennifer J. Griffin, Raymond C. Baumhart S.J. Endowed Professor of Business Ethics and Professor of Strategy, Quinlan School of Business, Loyola University, Chicago

"This book puts capitalism in an historical, cultural and political context. Financialised capitalism of the Reagan Thatcher era blew up in 2008. The argument for a new social contract between business and society in the future has to be answered."

Peter Folkman, Honorary Professor, Alliance Manchester Business School

"Millions of private companies are what makes capitalism work around the world, and this book is challenging them to step up to a new role in helping humanity face the next generation of economic, social and above all environmental problems."

Joanne Parker, COO, Chime Group

Acknowledgements

This book is derived from a lifetime of experience and many people have influenced the thinking set out here. Among them are my many former colleagues at Levi Strauss & Co and various consulting clients, including Mandy Cormack of Unilever, Neil Makin of Cadbury, Charlotte Grezo of Vodafone, Kathy Pickus and Jenna Daugherty of Abbott and Peter Heng of Golden Agri-Resources. There are many more in the business world struggling with the issues discussed here, just as there are in my former consulting company, where Mike Tuffrey, Amanda Jordan, Peter Truesdale, Helen Rushton, Esther Toth and others in the company have all said and done things to influence my thinking.

I am also indebted to many writers and thinkers on a wide range of topics from different fields of study; many of them are quoted and referenced in the text. In addition, I have benefited from the work of Professor David Grayson, formerly of Cranfield University; Jane Nelson at the Kennedy School of Government, Harvard University; and Jenn Griffin of Loyola University, Chicago; who have contributed to my understanding of corporate responsibility and sustainability.

Special thanks are due to Peter Folkman, whose comments about my first book on corporate citizenship inspired me to think more broadly about my audience and write this book. More specifically, in relation to the production of this book, I am indebted to Belinda Powell and Sarika Breeze, who both read it in detail and offered advice about key issues and the presentation of the contents. So too has Tim Ball who, as a solicitor, made some telling points about the text. My thanks go also to my wife, Gaye Logan, who has put up with me writing the book and made helpful suggestions.

Lastly, special thanks are due to Mindy Gibbins-Klein of Panoma Press, who read the book and creatively challenged aspects of my approach. Thanks also to her team, who helped produce and market the book. The publishing team all do a wonderful job.

Contents

Introduction

This book is being written at the height of the Covid-19 crisis around the world. Big government is back, just as it was following the banking crisis in 2008–09. This will tempt many to think that government is the answer to the world's problems, but it is not. As a result of the pandemic, there may well be some changes to how we organise society and the economy on a day-to-day level, but the fundamental organisation of a society, as explored in this book, will not change. Government will always have a vital role to play in shaping humanity's future, but governments cannot do it alone: they are only one type of social institution. The for-profit and non-profit sectors that have emerged around the world in recent years embody many more, and these institutions need to be included in the processes of shaping humanity's future.

Those of us born just after the second world war have lived through an extraordinary period of economic and social history, during which a sustained effort was made to run societies by government alone. Communism set out to eliminate capitalism, or at least to curtail it seriously, as well as the independent, citizen-based organisations of the non-profit sector. Millions died in the pursuit of the communist vision of a society free of economic 'exploitation' by a self-serving capitalist class, yet today capitalism is present in various forms in almost every society on the planet. Indeed, in the past 40 years or so it has become the driving force of our global economy.

There are many reasons why this great change has happened. Although this book does examine some of the reasons why capitalism won, it cannot explore them all in depth. Rather it asks the key question: if capitalism is back in such force, how can humanity work with it to address the economic, social and environmental issues of today and of the future? This book is not about replacing capitalism as an economic system; instead, it tries to understand capitalism, along with the constituent companies that make it work, to show how they could become positive agents for change, in conjunction with governments and an emerging non-profit sector.

The book does not suggest that this approach can 'save the world'. However, it does argue that since we have called capitalism back into being on a worldwide basis, we should charge its companies with a distinct role, beyond their commercial one, to help develop society and protect the natural environment. The book illustrates a very pragmatic and practical approach to shaping humanity's future. It is based on the idea of working more effectively with the institutions that humanity has organically developed, rather than trying to replace them with theoretically ideal ones.

We have not yet properly dealt with our recent past and learned its lessons. For example, there are many who still yearn for a 'socialist' type of revolution and argue that what happened in Russia in 1918 was not a 'real' revolution and that proper socialism has never been tried. Be that as it may, they still have to face the fact that communist and socialist regimes of all types – from Cambodia, East Germany, Cuba, India and the gentle social democracy of Sweden – have either collapsed or have been in retreat in the face of the enormous growth of 'free market values, resurgent capitalism and independent non-profit organisations.

Consequently, it is vital that we look more closely and in detail at the 'capitalist system' to see what humanity wants from it and how the system needs to be reformed in light of the world's current and future problems. Humanity has invited capitalism, and the private companies that make it work, back into the mix of social institutions around the planet, and we need to know how to live with it better.

Chapter 1 looks at the hugely important anti-capitalist movements of the 19th and 20th centuries, led by communists, socialists and other organised forces in society. It also points out that there is a general hostility to capitalism in certain segments of society, which limits our ability to engage in the creative discussion of the role of capitalism in shaping humanity's future.

Chapter 2 shows that private companies as economic and social institutions have been around since the beginning of recorded history and have existed in many diverse cultures. It looks at the history of capitalism, and at some of the reasons why it was hated by so many, but so attractive to others, and has consequently been brought back into our mix of social institutions. It also starts to identify the key role played by individual companies in developing capitalism and seeks to move the discussion somewhat away from the 'capitalist system' in general towards the role of individual companies and how they behave in society.

style

Chapter 3 identifies private companies as one of the primary types of social institution to be found around the world. It looks at the rise of the non-profit and for-profit sectors, and then looks at how the three formal sectors interact with each other and the informal sector of society. It looks at how society is organically evolving and developing around the world, as the state has retreated from economic and social dominance since the 1980s. It starts to argue that we must embrace these three evolving social sectors and learn to work with them to shape the future.

With the UK as the example, it also shows just how dominant the private sector is in the working life of a country, and it goes on to suggest that companies have a distinct capacity to act for good or ill. Even within the existing legal framework that governs them, companies play a key role in shaping the future of society, and that role can be developed for the common good.

style **Chapter 4** makes the case that we live in a very different world from the one that produced the Marxist critique of capitalism in the 19th century and that individual companies must urgently respond to these changes. It points out that since the 1980s we have come to recognise that humanity faces an immense global environmental crisis, and that private sector companies are critical in addressing it. Socially, today's better educated population is not deferential, and companies cannot just rely on the values of an inspired business leader as they have so often done in the past. All company stakeholders and wider society need to be actively engaged in what companies do to promote the common good.

Style This being the case, **Chapter 5** argues that society now needs to create a new social contract with private companies. We need to rewrite the legal framework that governs them and require all companies to have a commitment to social and environmental responsibility. This new obligation will be given in return for companies being allowed the freedom to continue to do what they do well in a free market, capitalist system. Companies can no longer be seen as purely private institutions pursuing private profit, and this change in law will give them, like governments and the non-profit sector, an obligation to consider and promote the public good. In future we must place on companies an obligation to use their abilities consciously to help humanity face the great issues of our time.

Many companies will object to this expansion of their legal obligations, but they need to know that responsible behaviour doesn't necessarily have to cost lots of money; in fact, it can sometimes help improve the business. However, there are times when doing the right thing can be expensive for a company and then it is vital for it to have the right values in place to help it make those difficult decisions that are of wider benefit to society. The issues humanity faces, particularly in respect of the natural environment, are just too pressing for businesses not to be legally obliged to play their part in addressing them.

style **Chapter 6** looks in detail at the two primary ways that companies can help with social development and environmental conservation: first, as a distinct institution in society; and second, in helping the company's stakeholders to be good citizens. Using the food industry as an example, it shows how many problems with capitalism can be addressed directly by socially and environmentally aware companies, and how such activities can positively and meaningfully change the day-to-day experience of capitalism for ordinary people.

The chapter also acknowledges that there are many issues in the capitalist system that individual companies cannot resolve. There will always be grounds for criticising the economic and social system that is developing around the world, and the role of private companies is a key part of this. On the other hand, the economic and social system has the virtue of being one which humanity seems to want, and which includes private companies. Consequently, we need to find a way for these companies to play their part, alongside the two other formal sectors and the informal sector, in facing the great problems of our day.

style This book is not motivated by anger at the capitalist system; neither is the book accepting of the kind of free market triumphalism that has been so prevalent since the fall of the Berlin Wall. Rather, it accepts the reality of humanity's choices in the social institutions it creates and tries to show how we can make the institutions that we have created organically work together better. This can be done only by firmly bringing private companies into a dialogue about humanity's future and they need to be prepared to do that.

style The book represents a different way of looking at capitalism. It does not ignore overarching issues with the capitalist system, such as the problem of economic inequality, but focuses on the individual companies that make the system work and their potential for making a positive contribution to humanity's progress. It also suggests that companies must, on many issues, be brought into alliance with the government and the burgeoning non-profit sector. As the price of their freedom to operate, they must join the other two organised sectors and systematically contribute to the public good.

The book does not seek to close the debates that will go on about the role of capitalism in society, but offers a way of engaging private companies in addressing a wide range of issues that would do much to make capitalism more acceptable to ordinary people. All too often commentators, particularly environmentalists and those on the left, argue that we must totally change society or change the whole economy, but offer few, if any, practical steps to achieve this. The communists tried and failed to create wholesale change; this book offers some examples of the much-needed practical steps in a pragmatic process of change that society needs, and tries to show how it might be achieved by collaboration between the three organised sectors of society.

The private for-profit sector and the non-profit sector now have to be recognised as vital components of society, along with the government, and that their very different knowledge, skills and special capacities can be utilised for the common good. Three perspectives are better than one and, with their different ways of interacting with the informal sector, the three formal sectors together can effect changes that will make a real, practical contribution to the future of humanity and the planet.

Lastly, when the communist movement began, it was looking to create a completely new world order, one without capitalism, private firms and charitable organisations. We have in the past few decades abandoned that vision and instead invited private enterprise back into the global mix of human institutions. Consequently, while the great issue of my young life was dominated by the question, "Should capitalism exist?" today the answer is clearly, "Yes!" So the question for the young of today is, "How do we live with it?"

I hope this book starts to give them and the public some clues to as to how the debate can be taken forward.

CHAPTER 1

The Great Global Debate

Introduction

The great political question of my young life from the 1950s until the late 1980s was, "Should capitalism exist?" Many societies around the world, including those in Russia and China, had said categorically no. These countries based their economy and society on the idea that capitalism and private enterprise must be eliminated. Others, such as India and Sweden, wanted it tightly controlled under socialist if not communist regimes. Similarly, in postwar Britain, the Labour party supported the idea of growing the economic power of the state through the progressive nationalisation of private firms, and I personally supported the labour movement and this broad approach. We need to remember that after the second world war, the large majority of the world's people lived in societies where capitalism had either been eliminated or was firmly under control of the state.

Throughout the 18th, 19th and 20th centuries, capitalism was so hated by millions that the ideas of the worldwide communist and socialist movements took a firm hold. From the success of the Russian Revolution in 1917, a sustained effort was made to eliminate free enterprise and capitalism from the world. The communist vision was a giant experiment in living, which aspired to a new future for humanity based on a world without capitalism and private enterprise.

Humanity has lived through a remarkable period of history when these two systems of economic and social thought violently clashed, so it is worth being precise as to what we are talking about. The *Oxford Dictionary of English* defines communism as:

> a theory or system of social organization in which all property is owned by the community and each person contributes and receives according to their ability and needs.

Webster's New Collegiate Dictionary goes into more detail, defining communism as:

> a theory advocating elimination of private property... a totalitarian system of government in which a single authoritarian party controls state-owned means of production with the professed aim of establishing a stateless society... a final stage of society in Marxist theory in which the state has withered away and economic goods are distributed equitably.

For many years, these sounded like very good ideas to many, but today the communist experiment has clearly failed, and capitalism is back as a major force in human affairs worldwide. Humanity needs to understand why this happened, because the worldwide opposition to capitalism was of extraordinary importance; there was almost a nuclear war fought over the matter, but the conflict has quietly passed into history as though it never happened.

On the other side of the clash was capitalism, which the *Oxford Dictionary of English* defines as:

> an economic and political system in which a country's trade and industry are controlled by private owners for profit, rather than by the state.

Webster's New Collegiate Dictionary again gives more detail in its definition of capitalism as:

> an economic system characterized by private or corporate ownership of capital goods, by investments that are determined by private decisions rather than by state control, and by prices,

production and distribution of goods that are determined mainly by competition in a free market.

Neither of these sets of definitions is extensive in terms of the detailed provisions of each system but they help set up the basic conflict of ideas between the two systems that dominated the world during the cold war years.

North Korea is one of the few countries that still rigidly follows communist ideas, but the country is one of the world's most backward; it has famines that have killed hundreds of thousands, and appalling levels of political repression and human rights abuses. The failure of the communist vision and the resurgence of capitalism have not been fully understood and appreciated. The failure of communism is not discussed much and to many it seems to have just faded away, like a bad dream. For free market thinkers, 'normal' life has been re-established, it seems, for the foreseeable future at least, and few from either camp have reflected on what recent history has taught us. However, we really do need to learn from this recent global history in order to shape humanity's future in a more ethical and sustainable way.

Today, capitalism and the private companies that drive it are at the heart of humanity's growing global economic and social systems and the question is not whether capitalism should exist, as it has kept emerging as a force in society since the beginning of recorded history. The question now is, "How do we learn to live with it? How do we accept that capitalism is here to stay and retain the benefits it brings while making it more socially responsible and environmentally sustainable?" These are the questions addressed in this book.

The world has never been so tightly integrated, by ease of trade, communication and travel; as the financial crisis and Covid-19 have shown. As our global society continues to grow and become more integrated, humanity is increasingly facing common problems, and capitalism is central to many of them. It is important, therefore, that we look in some depth at the role of free market enterprises in confronting them. But first it is worth looking at why capitalism was so reviled by previous generations and is still so distrusted today.

Growing Up With Socialism

I was born in a small Nottinghamshire mining village in 1947 (the year that India gained independence from Britain, and around the time when the Communist party seized power in China). My early life was lived against a background of socialist ideas, which forcefully advocated growing the power and size of the state and eliminating, or at least constraining, the role of private enterprises in society, often by taking them into public ownership. It was a worldwide intellectual trend, which had first begun to find practical expression in 1917, when the Marxist-inspired Communist party fought for and took control of the Russian state. From then on, with few exceptions, (most notably the US), leftist and big government ideas led the world's intellectual and political life, particularly in emerging and developing countries.

In the UK, this trend was clearly seen under the postwar Labour government of Clement Attlee, elected in 1945 as the second world war ended. This government drew on the wartime experience of the coalition government taking almost total control of the economy and it set out to create a new 'socialist' society. It quickly took large swathes of private industry into public ownership and created a coherent welfare state, with free healthcare and educational provision at its heart. Welfare benefits for unemployment and sickness were also created, and large numbers of publicly owned houses were built. We as young children were taken to the village hall to be weighed, vaccinated and given health checks, then given our orange juice and cod liver oil, as part of a plan to create a happier, healthier Britain. Mr Attlee aspired to a far greater degree of social justice and equality of opportunity than the old free market system had delivered.

We grew up believing in 'democratic socialism'. While not a communist society, the UK moved decisively left towards becoming a social democratic country in the western European style. Generally, we Labour supporters did not want to live in a totalitarian society like communists in Russia and China: rather we aspired to be like Sweden. In Sweden, nearly 70% of gross domestic product (GDP) was controlled by the state and the economy and social system were to be run for the benefit of all, not just a capitalist elite. There were some private enterprises in Sweden, such as the car manufacturer, Volvo, but even that seemed to be run with a view to fitting in with the values of society at large. For example, Volvo was renowned for its efforts to make life on the production line more creative and fulfilling for its workers, unlike the Ford Motor Company plant at Dagenham in the UK, which was embroiled in endless industrial disputes in the 1960s and 70s.

Socialism and communism were not just protest movements against past economic and social injustice; they were also seen as the harbingers of a much more just and efficient way of running an economy and developing a society. Leaving aside the social injustices communism was to redress, the economic central planning on which it was based was seen as a vastly superior system of wealth creation and distribution. When Nikita Khrushchev (first secretary of the Communist party of the Soviet Union) visited the US in 1959, his basic message was that communism was a superior form of economic organisation and production that would in time "bury" the wasteful capitalism of the west.

After all, the Soviets had created their own nuclear weapons shortly after the US and were the first to put a satellite, then a man, into space. In addition to Soviet technological achievements, social life was greatly enhanced through education, healthcare and other public services that were seen as manifestly good. New dams, canals, railways, mines, factories and coal-fired power stations were springing up everywhere in socialist economies and it seemed right and proper that the economy should be run to benefit all, not just the owners of capital.

The high point of these ideas was probably around the student revolt in Paris in 1968, when we really thought that socialism, and perhaps even communism, would triumph in France and large swathes of western Europe. By the end of the 1970s, however, Margaret Thatcher had been elected prime minister of the UK and she began to change the narrative of social and economic progress. By 1989, the Soviet system had collapsed with the Berlin Wall and there was a wholesale collapse in communist and leftist thinking. The notion of capturing the state by revolution in the case of Russia and China, or through the ballot box as in the UK, and using that power of the state to control the economy and consciously develop society, had run out of steam. Or very largely so.

The Power of the Communist Vision

The Communist Manifesto,[1] published in 1848, offered a critical turning point in the critique of capitalism, and even today it is a document worth reading. It was based on the large body of intellectual work by Karl Marx pointing towards a new world order where the injustice of inequality and economic exploitation was overturned. In many ways, *The Communist Manifesto* was a practical analysis of society and a cry of moral outrage as to how it was organised. Western society was seen to be sustaining the wealth of the few while actively promoting exploitation of the workers, who were creating the wealth.

It was also a manifesto for economic and social change based on seizing control of all means of production owned by the capitalist class and eliminating them, sometimes physically. Drawing on a long history of slave and peasant revolts against exploitation, communism was essentially a movement in response to the massive impact of private capitalism as it developed in Europe from the 17th century.

This was a time when Europe's first proto-multinationals emerged: the Dutch, French and British companies that began trading with Asia from the early 1600s. Over time, they were to spearhead the steady expansion of European colonialism (India was conquered by the British East India Company, not the British state), which continued in different forms right up to the early 20th century. European colonialism and capitalist enterprise have been intimately connected from the earliest days, and in the postwar years newly independent countries such as India, Vietnam, Ghana and Jamaica were consequently much more drawn to the socialist rather than the free market approach to the economy. They had many social problems to confront and saw international capitalism as the primary driver of their years of conquest and exploitation.

The connection between private enterprise and European colonialism cannot be overstated. It was so often private companies that penetrated the countries of Africa and Asia in particular; first as traders and then subsequently promoting state intervention to protect trade and property rights. These early companies saw the world as an open market and a great source of raw materials and labour, and there were few if any rules to constrain them. Once the former colonies had shaken off foreign rule, they were keen to nationalise or otherwise control the activities of foreign companies operating on their soil. Socialism went hand in hand with many independence movements, not least because many of the leaders of these movements had been educated in the anti-capitalist environment of European universities.

In addition to capitalism's impact on many countries around the world, the Industrial Revolution, led by capitalist entrepreneurs in Europe, took workers from the fields and put them in new factories and cities, with appalling conditions at work and at home. Karl Marx and Friedrich Engels were living in the UK at that time and saw at first hand this economic and social reality. They responded to the emergence of these new social conditions with their brilliantly argued critique of laissez-faire capitalism, equating mass poverty for the many with the exploitation of workers by a few wealthy owners of capital and land. *The Communist Manifesto* was a vision of a better society, which was to inspire generations of fervent anti-capitalists and led to the founding of new societies in the 20th century, in Russia, China and many other countries.

The communist vision was based on the elimination of most forms of private enterprise, the very foundation stone of the capitalist system, and the creation of a classless society. Among other things, *The Communist Manifesto*[2] argued for:

> Abolition of property in land and the application of all rents of land to public purposes.

> Abolition of all rights of inheritance.

> Centralisation of credit in the hands of the State, by means of a national bank with State capital and an exclusive monopoly.

> Centralisation of the means of communication and transport in the hands of the State.

> Extension of factories and instruments of production owned by the State.

> Free education for all children in public schools. Abolition of children's factory labour in its present form.

Communism rejected European laissez-faire capitalism and sought to take the ownership of capital and all the means of production out of the hands of private owners and companies. They were to be held in common by the state. In addition, the removal of the private entrepreneur and business owner would free workers from the alienation that naturally followed from working for a private employer and not being your own boss. For mainstream communists, the state was the instrument of liberation and would take complete control of the economy and develop society in a rational, planned and humanistic way. This was so that each individual would develop their full potential as a human being and that wealth would be created more effectively and distributed fairly. Capitalism and the private companies that were integral to it were seen as the enemy of human development and progress, therefore needed to be eliminated.

Why Did the Communist Project Fail?

The reaction of communism and socialism to the excesses and economic exploitation of 18th, 19th and 20th century capitalism is understandable, but why did this great revolutionary movement fail and what can we learn from that failure? Few leftists seem to have written about this problem and across the political spectrum there are many competing views of why the vison failed. This book cannot evaluate them all, since, not surprisingly, they vary depending on the commentator's point of view. Some say that the military challenge to the Soviet Union orchestrated by the US president, Ronald Reagan, put tremendous economic pressure on the Soviet system and helped to break down the economy. Others argue that in communist countries young people and ordinary people were rebelling against communist totalitarianism, where state control of the economy had metamorphosed into highly repressive regimes.

States such as Russia, East Germany and China did indeed give ordinary people little if any freedom in pretty much any aspect of life. Writers, poets and artists were repressed and spied on by an extensive secret police apparatus because they struggled to articulate the truth of their people's experience. Freedom of expression was a key aspiration for those inside the communist system. There were also the national aspirations of countries tied into the Soviet empire, and of course many argue that the enticements of the 'shallow' consumerist lifestyle of the west played a big part. Many more reasons were espoused for the failure of the communist experiment, but from the perspective of this book and the revival of capitalism, one issue stands out above all others.

At the heart of the problem for the communists was the claim that the new system would make people better off; that in short it would make them richer. When fully organised, communism would produce more goods, services and experiences for the mass of the people than capitalism ever could. Not only was the system supposed to be morally superior to that of the west, and the US in particular, but also much more productive. It did well when producing armaments, but that was not the case when it came to consumer goods.

Despite being dismissed as shallow desires by some commentators, many consumer goods – such as phones, fridges and cars – are important to people in everyday life. Communism was intensely restrictive and failed to give the people under its control the things they wanted and felt they needed to live a full life. As the communist atheists argued, you have only one life. People concluded that you had better enjoy it, and whatever is said about consumer goods and experiences, they can really help.

While communism gave the people some important things, including secure employment, free education, healthcare and greater emancipation for women, it did not give them what the western capitalist economies offered. It did not give them the freedom of thought, speech and movement, and above all it did not provide the goods and services that ordinary people wanted to enrich their personal lives. There was only so much that people would sacrifice for the 'project' and the state; they had their own lives to live and wanted the freedom for themselves and their children to live life more fully. Freedom of thought and the rule of law were important, but so was the desire to consume the range of goods and services at the relatively low prices that the free-market capitalist economies were offering.

If at the height of the cold war in the mid-1950s a Martian had visited Earth and been asked to judge which was the best system for humanity to live under, capitalism or communism, rather than relying on a theoretical debate, the visitor might have suggested a practical experiment to judge the question over 50 years or so. A wise Martian could have then selected a few countries around the world and divided them in half, such that one half was to develop under communism and the other under capitalism. At the end of the 50 years, the Martian might well have been able to judge which half of the country had done the best job of helping people live their lives well. A practical not a theoretical approach to the problem.

This is pretty much what happened during the cold war. In Asia, we have North Korea and South Korea; in Europe, East Germany and West Germany; and in the western hemisphere, the US and Cuba. It is not possible here to provide a detailed account of the comparative development of these different countries, although that would be helpful. However, there is still much that can be learned from their different experiences, and what stands out from the point of view of this book is not just the property rights, democracy, free press and relative personal freedom to be found in liberal capitalistic societies, but that during the cold war, the capitalistic countries gave their people the 'stuff', the consumer goods, they wanted in order to develop their lives. Everything was made available to the people: abundant food, books, films and TVs, credit cards, fashionable clothes, washing machines and cars, plus foreign holidays and the freedom to move around the world at will.

Communist countries were not insensitive to consumer desires and in many respects tried to meet them. So the East Germans, for example, created the poorly performing Trabant car for their people while the West Germans offered theirs a range of choices. That capitalist society offered the Volkswagen (initially developed by the Nazis as a people's car but it didn't make it to the market before the outbreak of the second world war, when production was halted), the Mercedes Benz, the BMW and the Audi at prices that even people on modest incomes could afford. West German TV was beamed into East Germany, where people could see how their counterparts lived; their revulsion at the communist regime exploded in 1989 when the Berlin Wall came down and they flooded across that barrier to experience life in the west.

North Korea turned into a complete totalitarian state run by the same family that founded it after the second world war. Today it has a very low standard of living, with periodic famines and a political and economic system totally controlled by the state. Consequently, and despite the great risks involved, a huge black market has developed as the people seek to get hold of western products such as videos. By comparison, South Korea, despite problems with authoritarianism and corruption, has offered its people a richer, fuller life. North Korea's GDP was estimated at around $40bn in 2015 ($1,700 per capita), while South Korea's GDP was estimated at around $1.92tn ($37,600 per capita). South Korea joined the Organisation for Economic Co-operation and Development (OECD) in 1996 and is considered a developed country, while North Korea still needs large amounts of external aid to survive.

In 1959, when Fidel Castro seized power in Cuba, like all communists he instituted a 'planned economy', designed to meet the needs and wants of the people, choosing not to develop the country in the organic and somewhat chaotic manner of the capitalist system and its 'exploitative elite'. Even though Cuba started from a low base compared with the US, by 2017 its GDP was estimated at $96.8bn ($8,540 per capita), whereas the US had a GDP of $19.39tn ($59,530 per capita). While Cuba has made less progress in terms of GDP per capita, it has made progress on the Human Development Index in terms of literacy and life expectancy, (GDP is not the only measure of progress, but an important one nonetheless). Its universal education and healthcare systems (which the US still does not have) have helped greatly in this respect and they show that not everything the communists did was a failure: their system did much for the emancipation of women, for example.

None of this is to say that countries that took a more capitalistic road during the cold war don't have their problems: they do. The US is one of the world's most capitalistic countries and it clearly struggles with race relations, economic inequality, healthcare provision and the performance of its education system. However, the idea that government-dominated, planned economies would solve pretty much all human problems has died the death. One of the great problems for the communist planned economy was that it received no signals from the marketplace as to what goods and services people wanted in their lives. Even if the people, as consumers, did send such signals to the planners, they were often ignored in communist societies primarily focused on workers as producers, not people as consumers.

What was on offer to the people in communist societies was what the party elite thought they should have. They tended to put the emphasis on increasing production, infrastructure projects and social services, including education, childcare and healthcare. The communist party in these countries even planned for the masses to experience culture, but it was the party's decision as to what should be consumed in books and plays, and on the radio, TV, personal computers and mobile phones. It was hard for the communist elite of the time to accept that ordinary people wanted to do things with their lives that their government disapproved of. The people wanted to own a fridge, a TV, listen to rock'n'roll, wear jeans, go shopping and drive modern cars. As well as resenting the oppression of the system, they resented the poor quality and range of goods and experiences they were given as part of everyday life.

I am not advocating consumerism here, simply reflecting on my experience as a child in the 1950s and 60s watching my parents, who had grown up through the Depression and the scarcity of the war, bring a range of consumer goods into our sparsely furnished council house in a Nottingham mining village. My mother bought a high-quality Bush radio, an electric cooker to replace the coal-fired range, a fridge, a washing machine and a vacuum cleaner, all of which helped her life in the home. She also expanded the range of foods we ate and eventually got a TV, while my father bought a moped to travel to work instead of cycling for an hour on cold, wet winter mornings to do an eight or 10-hour shift in a factory.

As I have travelled around the developing countries in Asia, Africa and Latin America, I have seen lots of poor families doing the same thing as my own. They want to improve their everyday lives in similar ways, by getting better housing, obtaining a range of useful consumer goods, and having a richer diet to improve their health and make life more enjoyable. If this is consumerism, then I am all in favour of it. It is not the world of Rolex watches, fast cars and private planes. It is the everyday aspiration of ordinary, poor people for a better life and it can be found all around the world.

A market-based approach to allowing private companies to innovate in producing goods and services for consumption, at a moderate or low cost, was infinitely more effective and attractive than the one developed by the planned economies. In addition to the political and social control of communist societies, what these economies produced was so often dull and disappointing for ordinary consumers.

In very many ways the communists and socialists were reacting to the exploitation, hardships and colonialism of Victorian capitalism. A top-down, centralised economy with a clear social purpose seemed like a good idea at the time; especially when compared with the organic and ever-changing growth of free-market capitalism. However, the experiment failed, and despite all the criticism that could be mounted against capitalist enterprise, it has been invited back into our system of social organisation all around the world. Why? Because it is good at giving people what they want to live their lives better.

However, it must be said that the forcefulness of the communist challenge to the free-market system did in some part change capitalism. The very existence of communism and socialism helped make western pro-capitalist governments and business leaders more careful in ensuring good behaviour by businesses towards employees, consumers and society. It also helped develop a consensus in the west around the provision of various forms of welfare support for ordinary people, even in the US. The very threat of communism was a factor in constraining the kind of capitalism we had seen in the Victorian era, and with its passing an external constraint on the behaviour of companies around the world has been lifted.

China Pioneers a New Vision

By the fall of the Berlin Wall in 1989, the command economy and the deeply totalitarian state that ran it was finished (with a few exceptions, such as North Korea). A new mood had developed around the world that welcomed back the contribution of private enterprise to society. For westerners it was the economic and social revolution championed in the early 1980s by Britain's prime minister, Margaret Thatcher, and the US president, Ronald Reagan, that began to manifest this change of thinking about free-market economics. However, the re-emergence of a role for private enterprise in society actually began in communist China in 1978 when Deng Xiaoping introduced 'capitalism with Chinese characteristics'.

In the mid-1970s, while working at the British Trades Union Congress, I had a pen-friend who was a professor at the Institute of Marxist Leninism in Beijing and a staunch communist. When he came to London, we had lunch at the Quo Vadis restaurant in Soho so that he could visit the two small rooms upstairs where Marx had written *Das Kapital* while living in poverty. When my friend told me that he was seeking permission to live in Hong Kong, I was very surprised, but he explained that the rapid economic growth of the colony was something he needed to understand. He and some other Communist party leaders had for several years been looking across the narrow seas at Taiwan and Hong Kong and watching their economies grow many times faster than that of mainland China.

For his part, the Chinese leader Deng Xiaoping wanted to help his people improve their lives by promoting faster economic growth and to that end he was not above borrowing some of the creativity found in the private sector in these offshore territories. Once the remains of the Maoist Cultural Revolution had finally been swept away, the Chinese Communist party began backing away from the command economy and encouraging private enterprise. When Deng came to power, nearly 100% of all workers in the formal economy worked for the state, whereas today it is about 22%. Hundreds of millions are now working in various forms of private enterprise, some government-owned and many funded by government banks, but free of detailed state control.

Since 1978 and the Deng reforms, the Chinese economy has been growing at an unprecedented rate of nearly 10% a year. China has succeeded in lifting an estimated 850 million of its people out of extreme poverty (defined by the World Bank as living on $1.90 a day or less per person); its extreme poverty rate has declined from over 80% of the population in the 1970s to about 1% today. Experts think that this export-led growth will decline somewhat as economic priorities shift towards promoting even greater domestic consumption, but the point is made. By adopting aspects of capitalism, the Chinese Communist party supercharged the economic growth of a largely rural country while still retaining political power.

The Chinese Communist party has not adopted western democracy, a free press, an independent judiciary or the activist non-profit organisations that are a critical part of western society, but it has adopted key aspects of economic capitalism to secure economic growth. Most notably, it has devolved a certain amount of economic power to independent private firms in order to supply local and international markets. The communist project, as an economic one at least, is over in China and it remains to be seen whether the political and cultural institutional structures typical of western versions of capitalism, including political democracy, will follow.

The Chinese Communist party, like many other communists and socialists around the world, has acknowledged that its economic system, supposed to be a superior form of production to capitalism, was flawed, and it has made pragmatic changes accordingly. Despite a long history of antipathy towards indigenous and western capitalist enterprises (the East India Company started the first of the destructive opium wars with China), China had to allow key elements of capitalism back into society to achieve economic growth and social change. While that has solved some problems for the country, it has introduced others, such as serious wealth inequality, new forms of corruption and substantial growth in highly polluted cities.

The Impact on Western Socialists

From the 1980s, there was a worldwide shift in mood about the role of private business in society, and countries of all political persuasions started to create more space for private companies to function. Not only was communism in retreat, but socialists of various types also had to adapt. Socialism is defined in the *Oxford Dictionary of English* as:

> A political and economic theory of social organization which advocates that the means of production, distribution and exchange should be owned or regulated by the community as a whole. Policy or practice based on this theory. (In Marxist theory) a transitional social state between the overthrow of capitalism and the realization of Communism.

Even in Sweden, the doyen of socialist democracies in the 1970s and 80s, the socialist government had to retrench. The Swedish government's socialist aspirations had grown progressively over this period until government spending as a share of the country's GDP reached 70%. By the early 1990s, however, a financial crisis brought an end to the approach based on tax-and-spend policies, and in 1996 Sweden put a cap on public spending. The country went on to abolish inheritance tax in 2005 and wealth taxes in 2007, and since 2010 government spending has been equal to around 50% of the country's GDP. The top rate of tax in Sweden is now about 57% of an individual's income, not far out of line with the high-tax US state of California. Like the communists, the social democrats realised that they could not run a country without a vigorous private sector to pay the bills.

Other western countries, including the UK, also adapted and became much more accepting of private enterprise and capitalism. In the 1980s, Margaret Thatcher denationalised industries, privatised companies such as British Petroleum, British Airways and British Telecommunications, sold off public housing and then cut personal taxes, all the time championing private enterprise and individual initiative. In the US, Ronald Reagan, took a similar path to Mrs Thatcher's by cutting taxes, confronting trades union power and stimulating the private sector economy. The social democratic left, like the communists, had to accept that the days of big government were over, for the foreseeable future at least. They too had to accept that capitalism, the motives that drove it and the companies that made it work, had to be recognised as part of society's future.

In the UK, Mrs Thatcher's revolution had run out of steam in 1997 when Tony Blair's Labour party won a landslide victory, but the New Labour government barely touched the Thatcher reforms. Indeed, under Tony Blair's leadership in 1995 and before its election victory, the Labour party ditched the famous clause IV of its constitution,[3] which had previously committed it to red-blooded socialism:

> To secure for the workers by hand or by brain the full fruits of their industry and the most equitable distribution thereof that may be possible upon the basis of the common ownership of the means of production, distribution and exchange, and the best obtainable system of popular administration and control of each industry or service.

In 1999 Peter Mandelson, New Labour's main strategist famously said of the party, "We are intensely relaxed about people getting filthy rich as long as they pay their taxes." It was a comment made in California to an audience of technology company executives and was in effect the formal 'surrender' of the social democratic left to the resurgence of capitalism in the west. Labour knew it could never get elected if it put forward the old strategies of state control of the economy and high taxes. Mandelson was acknowledging that capitalism would lead to greater inequalities of wealth, but so long as the rich paid their taxes, the soft left could still use government spending to change society through the education, health and welfare systems.

Before it ended in 2007 when Gordon Brown took over as prime minister, Tony's Blair's government did make a small attempt to shape the behaviour of the companies that make up the capitalist system by including a section in the 2006 Companies Act that asked them to behave with a regard to the company's stakeholders and wider society. Section 172 of the Act requires directors of companies to act in good faith and pay regard to the long-term consequences of their decisions, particularly for employees, other stakeholders and the environment. It was a gesture toward setting a new social contract between businesses and society, but not at all a forceful one. More about this issue in later chapters.

It was Margaret Thatcher and Ronald Reagan, politicians of the right, who recognised when they were giving business much more power and freedom to operate, that business needed to become more responsible and active in helping society face its issues. But the activism model they seem to have had in mind was one of companies doing more philanthropy and community engagement. This is essentially a 19th-century idea that has its value, but on its own is utterly inadequate for our modern times. In his Economic Renewal Act of 1981, for example, President Reagan raised the level that companies could give to charity to 10% of profits, but as far as I know no company ever did that.

In China, the Communist party felt that it could create a vast new private sector while keeping political control of society at large. In western countries, politicians of the left and right gave little thought to the effect of their policies in bringing back private enterprise to prominence in society. In many ways, it was for pro-business westerners a return to 'normality', and no one thought through what was to be required of the private companies that drive the capitalist system in the modern world. They are key to humanity's future and must be included in any attempt to address society's economic, social and environmental problems. The social democratic left is still divided between those who were ready to compromise with capitalism as it is, such as Tony Blair, and those who still wanted to seriously constrain and control it.

In the UK, the election of Jeremy Corbyn, a socialist, as leader of the Labour party showed that the traditional socialist left was still a force. The emergence of Bernie Sanders and Elizabeth Warren as 'democratic socialist' candidates for the leadership of the US Democratic party was another sign of how socialist ideas still find resonance today. The socialism of these left-leaning leaders is not as red-blooded as in previous generations, but it is alive and well (it is reported that Jeremy Corbyn flirted with the idea of reinstating clause IV of the Labour party's constitution). Despite a surge in support from very many young people for Mr Corbyn's election to the leadership, the party was roundly defeated at the general election in 2019. This was partly because of the party's position on Brexit and membership of the European Union, but also because the public rejected Mr Corbyn's 'socialistic policies' (including proposed nationalisations). Consequently, the general pattern of society incorporating a large private sector remains the economic reality of the UK, the US and most other countries around the world today.

Other Organised Opponents of Capitalism

Throughout history, communists and socialists have not been the only enemies of capitalism and free enterprise. Among these other enemies of capitalism in the 20th century who set out to capture the state and control private enterprise, two groups are of particular significance: first, far-right, nationalist politicians; and second, religious groups. The far right believed that the interests of the nation were far more important than any private enterprise and were willing to suppress companies that did not fit their world view. Religious groups have a view about the human behaviour that is acceptable to their God and have used the power of the state to ensure that private companies do not transgress important religious teachings. The most prominent and important of the two in the last century were the right-wing nationalists.

1. Right-Wing Nationalists

Like the political left, the political right is split into factions and while conservative leaders such as Margaret Thatcher and Ronald Reagan favoured free markets and free enterprise in principle, there was an element on the right that was hostile to capitalism because its international links, unruly creativity and other activities could be seen as damaging to national interests. The most extreme version of this view was held by the Nazi party (the Nationalsozialistische Deutsche Arbeiterpartei or the National Socialist Workers Party of Germany). Hitler hated what he called 'Jewish American capitalism' and sought to control the German economy and its private firms through the use of state power. While favouring certain companies that made armaments and promoted German autarky, the Nazis imposed wage, price and dividend controls on business and forced many companies to join state-managed cartels while readily putting others out of business.

In *The Wages of Destruction*,[4] Adam Tooze shows how companies that were to benefit from the Nazi war economy, such as Krupp, were early supporters of Hitler, while others, such as those in the textile industry, were suppressed because they were integrated into the global economy and did not help the Nazis build the nationalistic, economic autarky they were striving for.

When writing of Hitler's rise to power, after the Russian Revolution of 1917 had been consolidated and the world economy was in crisis, Adam Tooze says of German business:

> In the aftermath of World War 1, the business lobby had been strong enough to constrain the revolutionary impulses of 1918–19. Now capitalism's deepest crisis left German business powerless to resist a state interventionism that came not from the left but the right.

> The first years of Hitler's regime saw the imposition of a series of controls on German business that were unprecedented in peacetime history.

One of the many factors motivating some German business leaders to support the Nazis despite the enormous state intervention that was imposed by them, was the fear of their assets being expropriated if the communists took power. By supporting the Nazis, at least they got to keep some measure of control of their businesses and profits. National pride would have been another motive, and domestic companies no longer faced competition from international capitalism, which by its nature was 'cosmopolitan', bringing new and foreign ideas, people and products into the country. This aspect of global trade could threaten domestic industries just as it does today, and foreign-owned companies are easy targets for populists of the right as well as the left.

Populism and economic nationalism have often gone together, and in Latin America there is a long history of 'populist' political leaders who want to protect their country from foreign interference and foreign commerce. The Peronist movement in Argentina is one example, and in Brazil the Vargas presidency embodied a tradition of economic nationalism that was revived by the Argentinian president, Néstor Kirchner, in 2003, to be carried on by his wife Christina until 2015 when economic policy tended towards autarky. Hostility to big business, and international companies in particular, was widespread in the country, and the government positioned itself as defenders of the poor from the exploitation of the capitalist system, national and international.

Nevertheless, private firms have survived in these countries because they were essential to the continuation of the nation's economic life and because populists rarely seek to eliminate them, just to make them subservient to 'national interests' as they define them. This problem arises from the global economy and the three great and primary 'political' demands of international business, which have always been the free movement of goods, the free movement of capital, and the free movement of labour. There are lesser demands, such as lower taxes and less regulation, but the big three demands mentioned above can cause major problems for a particular country, and politicians of both the left and the right have been constantly active in opposing one or all of them.

2. Religious Groups

There is scope for a whole book about religion and business, but for the purposes of this one it is sufficient to note that all great religious traditions hold views about how business and commerce should be conducted and controlled. As the two great secular religions of the 20th century, communism and Nazism, have declined, there has been something of a resurgence in the importance of traditional religious teachings and how they relate to business today.

It is only in a few countries, such as Iran and Saudi Arabia, that real theocracies still exist today, and in these countries business activity is still regulated by religious belief. *The Holy Quran*, for example, is very specific about how business people should behave and much thought is given in Muslim countries, such as Malaysia, on how to reconcile religious teaching with the demands of the modern, international capitalist economy. However, in most Christian societies, religious traditions tend to influence people's general attitudes to business and capitalism, rather than provide detail about behaviour. This is done in many societies by shaping people's basic sense of 'fairness' and justice. Generally speaking, most scriptures and religious teachings require people, including business leaders, to act with concern for their fellow human beings.

Most religious traditions maintain their approach to business and the capitalist system by criticising how it works from a moral perspective. In the US, for example, Christian churches often question a company's management about how they treat their employees, suppliers and customers, and will take a lead on shareholder resolutions designed to change corporate behaviour.

Business is still treated with suspicion by many religious groups, in part because it is concerned much more with the physical reality and pleasures of life, not with the spiritual aspects. Consequently, religious thinkers view the world of commerce with concern; they see organisations operating in a narrow form of profitable self-interest, not for the public good or for the benefit of humanity generally. More broadly, in the Christian world where some theology says there are seven deadly sins (pride, lust, envy, greed, gluttony, sloth and wrath), there seem to be a whole range of businesses designed to promote and enable them (eg drinking, gambling, overeating, pornography, keeping ahead of the neighbours in consumption and, in the US, the sale of handguns).

Nevertheless, religion has influenced the attitudes of many business leaders, from many faiths, who take their values and religious ethics into their work. Generally speaking, however, business does not sit easily alongside religion. It has profits to make, employees and suppliers to deal with and consumers to serve by making lots of practical decisions, which have distinct implications for religious life around the world. Modern multinationals have therefore tended to try to be accommodating of religious differences by acting in a decidedly secular way and this in itself has raised problems for them. Companies have to accept and work with people's religious affiliations, if they are to be successful.

How Does Humanity Feel About Capitalism Today?

There are distinct groups of people, in western societies at least, who have attitudes that are hostile to business, moneymaking, materialism and consumerism, while not being in any way organised. Many have an attitude to life inherited from the 19th and 20th-century tradition of Bohemian artists, creatives and cultural commentators. In *Among the Bohemians*,[5] Virginia Nicholson says of the Bohemians:

> If poverty is an imperative for an artist – as many believed it to be – then wealth was to be derided, regarded as sordid and corrupting to the integrity of the artist. Bohemia on the whole felt a psychic distaste for Mammon.

There are many in the arts, academia and the media world who think that the only worthwhile things in life are those activities undertaken for their own sake and not for profit. Art, poetry, philosophy, music and literature are typical examples of this group's passion and there is a corresponding disdain for commerce and profit-making.

People loosely affiliated to this grouping are important in society because they greatly influence the public dialogue about society's future, especially through mass media. They are very influential in creating opinions about many aspects of life and society in which they can, directly or unknowingly, create a disdain for business and commerce as opposed to the higher motives of cultural creation that they pursue.

The point here is that it is not an either/or situation. The free-roaming creativity of cultural life is important and people need a cultural life as well as a practical and commercial one. However, there is no reason for the inheritors of the Bohemian tradition to disdain the everyday process of making a living through running a business and making a profit, not least because many in the arts, academia and the media are also trying to make a living and seeking to generate an income from their work.

Despite the resurgence of capitalism around the world, there is little hard evidence of how people now feel about it when comparing it with socialism, for example. Results from a Pew Research Centre poll in the US in 2019 showed that about 50% of under-49s had a positive impression of socialism, while 75% of people older than 65 had somewhat positive impressions of capitalism. There is definitely a split between the generations, in the west at least, as to how people feel about capitalism and socialism; the younger generation is much more inclined to be hostile to capitalism.

This may be in part because of the rise of the environmental movement over past decades. The doyen of the movement in Britain, the film-maker Sir David Attenborough, is quoted in *The Times*[6] in October 2020 as saying:

> The excesses the capitalist system has brought us have got to be curbed somehow. That doesn't mean to say that capitalism is dead. I'm not an economist and I don't know but I believe the nations of the world, the ordinary people worldwide, are beginning to realise that greed does not actually lead to joy.

It is not just environmentalists who have such views, however; there are many international non-profit organisations, such as Oxfam, which echo these sentiments in terms of the social inequalities and problems as well, and young people are much more inclined to actively support them.

Worldwide, one of the few global surveys that seek to address people's attitude to capitalism is prepared each year by the US-based Edelman public relations company. It gives us some clues. The Edelman Trust Barometer,[7] which is usually presented to world leaders and business people at the Davos retreat each year, covers 28 markets (mainly in developed and newly industrialising countries) and tests the opinions of over 34,000 opinion leaders and ordinary people around the world. The survey produced in October and November 2019 showed that of those surveyed, 56% agreed with the statement, "Capitalism as it exists today does more harm than good in the world." In 21 of the 28 markets surveyed, people were afraid of being left behind by the economy, and in 15 of them, people were pessimistic about their economic prospects.

The public discourse about capitalism is often conducted poorly, with lots of abstract and generalised comment. We need to unpick that discussion and recognise that capitalism has always had at least two major aspects that shape its presence in society: first, the economic creativity and ethical behaviour of its individual companies as agents of the market economy; and second, the overall impact of the system as a whole on society.

This book proposes that we start our reassessment of capitalism by looking first and foremost at the behaviour of the companies that drive capitalism. It suggests that by shaping the behaviour of the individual companies that make up the 'system' we can influence many, but not all, of capitalism's problems. We need to step back and try to look objectively at what capitalism offers humanity and why we want it, so that we can retain what is good about it and match that contribution with an obligatory commitment to social responsibility and environmental sustainability.

To set the scene for a discussion of these issues, the next chapter looks at the lengthy history of capitalism and the private companies that make it work. It briefly looks at the good and bad sides of the system and ponders what there is about it that has caused humanity to bring it back into the mix of social institutions we have around the world today. Capitalism and private business does have a long history and despite every attempt to supress it, the system survives. Also, it has come to dominate so much of the global economy and society that we have an obligation to better understand it and learn to work with it. Striving to abolish it in the way that the communists did is not the answer.

CHAPTER 2

Capitalism: It Is a Love-Hate Relationship

Style
Introduction

The first thing to realise about businesses, and even multinational companies, is that they have been part of human culture since the origins of recorded history. Private firms were one of the earliest and most successful forms of social organisation invented by humanity. Capitalism and private enterprise were not invented by Victorian Europeans; they have been around much longer.

In their article in the *Management International Review* in 1998, entitled 'The First Multinationals: Assyria Circa 2000 B.C',[8] Karl Moore and David Lewis use evidence from clay tablets found in the Iraqi desert to explore the activities of trading companies, multinational enterprises (MNEs) that operated there some 4,000 years ago.

> The definition of MNE accepted by the OECD and the UNTC, "an enterprise that engages in foreign direct investment (FDI) and owns or controls value-adding activities in more than one country"... leads us to conclude that there were MNEs in ancient Assyria around 2000 B.C. Characteristics found in modern MNEs such as: hierarchical organization, foreign employees, value-adding

activities in multiple regions, common stock ownership, resource and market-seeking behavior, were present in these ancient firms. These early MNEs successfully operated considerable business empires in multiple foreign locations from their corporate headquarters in the capital of Ashur.

They go on to ask whether there were even earlier examples of MNEs operating than those they have identified in Assyria, and conclude that it was possible, although there is a lack of archaeological evidence to prove the point. Moore and Lewis are talking about the emergence of formally organised 'companies' that have shareholders and staff and act at scale to organise trade and production over long distances. There is a mass of archaeological evidence, however, to show that 'commerce', manufacturing and trade existed for many thousands of years before the emergence of these formally constituted Assyrian businesses. Around 17,000 BCE, Stone Age people in Indonesia traded obsidian, which they used to make tools and arrowheads, while later in Europe flint was similarly manufactured and traded over a wide area.

In *Foundations of Corporate Empire: Is History Repeating Itself?*[9] Moore and Lewis trace the history of business and business organisations through the Phoenicians, Greeks, Romans, the Harappan civilisation of the Indus Valley, across the Muslim world and in Chinese society. They cite evidence of large-scale manufacturing and trading activity across various regions of the world. It was often led by local products, such as wine and the manufacture of containers to transport it. Business is not a modern invention; it is what humans have done throughout history and each era has had its examples.

So, the answer to the question in the title of Moore and Lewis's book is, "Yes!" History does repeat itself when it comes to creating business activity and the formation of companies to pursue it. It is what the human race does all around the world. For modern Europeans, a key moment came when in 1498 Vasco Da Gama finally reached India by ship, supplanting overland trade organised by Venice, and began the integration of European and Asian trade. That development was ultimately to be the foundation of our first global economy, initially through the activities of the great European charter companies, especially the Dutch East India Company, British East India Company and French East India Company. They were the harbingers of the modern capitalist world and their activities began to fuel the reaction against capitalism that culminated in the violent communist and socialist opposition discussed in the previous chapter.

Why Do Companies Exist?

Throughout history, the key driver for people doing business has been the desire of 'consumers' to possess the products that farming, manufacturing and trade brought them. Their reasons for obtaining these products were various. For example, a flint arrow or spear head, axe or cutting tool was more effective than the hardened wood alternative used in hunting for generations. These types of new tools did a job better and could be desirable for that reason alone.

But precious stones and artefacts, such as devotional statues, ceramics and fine fabrics, were a pleasure to possess, while wine and spices greatly increased the appeal of food. Life is for living, after all, and free enterprise in society brought forth many goods, and indeed services, that were very much to be desired. The consumer's desire for new, useful and attractive things, may also have endowed a particular consumer with greater status, something else that humans desire and another reason for welcoming trade.

The producers of the goods, on the other hand, could well have had a pride in the mastery of materials and products, such as creating bronze and turning it into fine weapons. But ultimately it was the desire of someone, somewhere, to possess what was created that drove the process. Goods and services are unlikely to be produced unless they are to be consumed; to respond to consumer demand, traders and producers had to organise companies to act at scale. This capacity to act at scale is the primary reason why companies are created.

Companies enabled entrepreneurs to grow to scale and pay suppliers, engage transport, make provision for difficult times, pay taxes and ultimately become wealthy. It was early in human history that business became established as a wealth-creating activity, distinct from that of the king, the government and landlords, whose wealth usually depended on the taxation of agriculture and trade. Business was able to create considerable wealth from the process of a voluntary exchange of goods and services between producers and consumers, and that reality has remained controversial throughout history to the present day.

How wealth is made and distributed by business activity is a question that has troubled free-market capitalism throughout time. From the earliest times, governments, kings and tribal leaders very often regulated the operations of economic enterprises for political and social reasons, but also to raise money by taxing them. However, as our recent history has shown, societies would from time to time overthrow the free-market system and the companies that were part of it, in part because the merchant class had become powerful or rich enough to threaten the established social order.

In *Babylon: Mesopotamia and the Birth of Civilization*,[10] Paul Kriwaczek points out that society is constantly trying different approaches to living and organising social and economic relations:

> … ancient Mesopotamia acted as a kind of experimental laboratory for civilization, testing, often to destruction, many kinds of religion, from early personifications of natural forces to full-blown temple priesthood and even the first stirrings of monotheism; a wide variety of economic and production systems from (their own version of) state planning and centralized direction to (their own style of) neo-liberal privatization, as well as an assortment of government systems, from primitive democracy and consultative monarchy to ruthless tyranny and expansive imperialism. Almost every one of these can be paralleled with similar features found in our own more recent history.

Long before the Greeks effectively started early European history, our ancestors in Mesopotamia were struggling with balancing the relative roles of business, government and religion in society and making radical changes to try to get the balance right. Human beings have, throughout history, constantly experimented with different forms of social organisation – such as private enterprises, various forms of government and religious and mutual organisations – in a struggle to find the right balance of social institutions to help people live their lives well. It is a repeating pattern of great significance in how society evolves.

It is clear, however, that the enduring factor of human desire, which drove consumption and private enterprise in the past, still drives it today. Even in societies such as that in North Korea, where private enterprise is totally forbidden, black market trading is endemic. The people of that country take immense risks to engage in various forms of illegal commerce. The desire of consumers to experience new goods and services through the marketplace remains a constant throughout history, as does the entrepreneurial desire to meet it.

The Early Modern Economy

It is worth looking in some detail at the emergence of activity in the early modern European economy, because people tend to think that it defines capitalism, and it is good to know why it provoked such immense hostility around the world. More specifically, early modern international capitalism in Europe probably began with the creation of a range of chartered companies, which began to trade around the world in the 16th century. Established by government charter in Britain, these companies included, for example, the Muscovy Company, founded in 1555, and the Turkey Company, founded in 1583. But possibly most important of all was the British East India Company, founded in 1600. The Dutch had their East India Company, the VOC, founded in 1602 while the French founded theirs in 1664, and they all fed an insatiable demand in Europe for rare spices and other goods, including fabrics and fine ceramics from around the world, but Asia and China in particular.

The British East India Company is a good example of a proto-modern multinational. It was a joint stock limited company, ultimately with many investors, that was given a monopoly of trade beyond the Cape of Good Hope and allowed to export bullion to purchase goods in Asia for resale in Britain and empire markets. In its earliest days, it tried to dominate the Indonesian spice trade because spices were highly prized and very profitable, and *Nathaniel's Nutmeg*,[11] a book by Giles Milton, details the battles fought between the forces of the Dutch East India Company and its British counterpart for the control of the very lucrative spice trade from Indonesia. The British company lost out to the Dutch and then focused its attention on India.

Over successive centuries, the company conquered most of the subcontinent. It was normal in those days for trading companies to maintain large navies and armed forces to protect their interests in countries where they traded and on the high seas. They also fought battles with each other for control of sources of raw materials and markets. The Hudson Bay Company, for example, fought a small but bitter battle in Canada with the competing Northwest Company in 1816 at what became known as the Seven Oaks Massacre.

The British East India Company, with the support of the British state, was able to launch the first Opium War with China (1839–41) when, in the name of free trade, it defied the Chinese state's attempts to control opium imports and their use. Opium had been in wide use in China for centuries, but in 1644 the newly established Qing dynasty began to try to control it. This brought the government of China into conflict with the British East India Company, which had established a monopoly of opium production in Bengal in 1793 and found a ready market for its high-quality products in China. By 1839, the company was exporting more than 40,000 chests of opium to China and generating huge profits in silver by doing so. That income in turn helped to cover the costs of an outflow of silver for other goods, such as tea, ceramics and fabrics that the company imported to the British and North American markets. The company saw the trade as a normal business activity in meeting consumer needs and wants.

While most people in Britain have forgotten about these events, they were dramatic and even today have left a deep imprint on the historical memory of the peoples of India and China. Consequently, these people remained very suspicious of foreign-owned multinationals and in the 19th and 20th centuries were willing to embrace a Marxist analysis of global economics. Today, international companies don't fight wars of conquest and instead compete with each other without violence (unlike nation states, ethnic groups and religious believers). What they do, which is what the British East India Company did in its day, is to serve their consumers by giving them whatever they want at prices they will pay. In past times, that included opium.

style
The Case of Capitalism and Cotton

The story of cotton shows why capitalist activities were welcomed in society and why they were hated by so many. The history of cotton is a more subtle example of how the British East India Company changed the world through trading rather than through conquests and military means. Furthermore, the growth and use of cotton still has a resonance in today's economy. History illustrates the impact of a multinational company based in Britain promoting the use of the wonderful cotton textiles to be found in India, to the great detriment of British cloth producers. This is described by Frank Trentmann in *Empire of Things*:[12]

> Cotton, however, was the first truly global mass consumer good … it was in England that they first reached the middling sort and then the masses. In 1664, the English East India Company (EIC) shipped a quarter of a million pieces of cloth to England. Twenty years later it shipped a million.

He goes on to say:

> Indian cottons threatened local wool, linen and silk industries, which led to a virtually European-wide ban on calico (France: 1689; Spain: 1713; Britain: 1700 and 1721; Russia: 1744); only the Netherlands stood apart. In Spitalfields, London, in 1719–20, women had their calico dresses torn off their backs by rioting silk weavers. But prohibition failed to kill the 'calico craze'...

In *The Travels of a T-shirt in the Global Economy*,[13] the economist Pietra Rivoli looks at the modern trade in cottons, but takes time to review at length the measures undertaken by the British state to protect the woollen industry, which had been the basis of English trade and wealth since the middle ages. She says of the struggle:

> The woollen weavers won the war, clearly and decisively. On December 25, 1722, it became illegal to wear or to use in home furnishings almost all types of cotton cloth. And the law was not a brief insanity. The ban on cottons would not be lifted for decades, forcing a generation of Britons into hot, itchy, and expensive clothing, all in the name of saving the domestic textile industry.

However, the law against cottons was hard to enforce. The workforce of the East India Company was involved in a great deal of smuggling calico over this period and it was not until 1774 that the ban on printed Indian cotton was rescinded. By this time, however, a domestic industry had developed using new technology and by 1800 the country was consuming about 30m yards of home-produced cotton cloth.

This conflict was an early example of a struggle between local producer communities and a multinational serving consumer demand by using overseas sources; and this remains a key issue today. As multinationals source goods and services from China and India, they put US and British workers, among others, out of jobs. So not all stakeholders benefit equally from the actions of a company, particularly one operating in the global economy, with all the opportunities that provides for the cheap sourcing of goods, services and labour from overseas. This fact is the source of much concern about modern capitalism too.

To complete the story, capitalist innovation in the local British cotton industry led it to become extremely productive, such that prices per piece of cloth dropped dramatically. The industrialised process of cotton manufacture first drove handloom weavers out of business in Britain and then began providing cheap cotton cloth to India; which in turn threatened the livelihoods of Indian handloom weavers. Their interests were championed by Mahatma Gandhi and the Congress party, which initially had a spinning wheel on its party flag; and Gandhi was often seen at a spinning wheel himself. Militant Indian nationalists burned cheap Manchester-produced cloth on the dockside in order to protect their village weavers and local markets from international business.

While entrepreneurial creativity and the Industrial Revolution experienced in Manchester and other cities brought down the price of cotton cloth and other goods, it also helped create terrible conditions in the factories that produced them and the cities that grew up around them. It was the direct experience of these conditions that did so much to inspire the work of Marx and Engels (whose family owned a textile factory in Manchester and knew it well). In addition, the cotton that sustained the Manchester factories increasingly came from North America where the raw material was produced by slaves; an early example of modern capitalism's willingness to exploit labour, a problem that continues to this day.

In *Empire of Cotton: A New History of Global Capitalism*,[14] Sven Beckert acknowledges that slavery was well established in the Caribbean and the US, producing products like sugar to sweeten tea from China and India, and tobacco and indigo, but with the opening of new lands in the US and the invention of the cotton gin, he says:

> In the thirty years after the invention of the gin alone (between 1790 and 1820), a quarter million slaves were forcefully relocated, while between 1783 and the closing of the international slave trade in 1808, traders imported 170,000 slaves into the United States – or one-third of all slaves imported into North America since 1619. Altogether, the internal slave trade moved up to a million slaves forcefully to the Deep South, most to grow cotton.

Given these examples of the impact of global capitalism from the 17th to the 19th century, it is no wonder that the Marxists and socialists wanted to abolish it and control it. They saw a few capitalists get rich while the mass of poor people and workers suffered dreadfully from the changes that capitalism brought about. In turn, the capitalist class saw a world open for business with little constraint and rushed forward to exploit the opportunities it presented, with scant regard for the impact their activities had on the masses, other than as consumers of their products. The class war that the Marxists advocated on behalf of the workers surged as an idea, and from then onwards the notion of capturing the state by revolution and using its power to eradicate capitalism became a global force of great power.

Companies in the Modern Economy

Modern capitalism has in part been revived around the world because the social, economic and political conditions under which it initially developed have now changed for the better, arguably in some large part due to the agitation of communists, socialists and progressives generally. The context for doing business locally and internationally is now different from what it was in the 18th and 19th centuries when the East India Company conquered India and sold opium to China. At that time, there were no agreed international standards of behaviour for businesses, such that what companies did in those times would be unthinkable today.

Forced colonisation, the use of slavery and child labour, for example, have been banned. Humanity has at last renounced such activities and said so in the United Nations (UN) Universal Declaration of Human Rights, first published in 1948. Standards have been codified and governments, many of them post-colonial states, representing the vast majority of the world's population, have signed up to them. The Universal Declaration of Human Rights sets global standards for the treatment of people worldwide and many companies have striven to comply with modern ethical and legal standards as they have developed their businesses locally and internationally.

In addition, a large number of international organisations have subsequently been created – including the UN Global Compact, the World Trade Organisation, the OECD and the International Labour Organisation (ILO) – to help set standards of behaviour and monitor corporate behaviour. The explosion of modern international communications such as television, the internet and the mobile phone has helped ensure companies' accountability for their behaviour. Gone are the days when it took more than six months for a letter from London to reach East India Company employees in Calcutta.

Today any state or corporate actor engaging in bad behaviour can be exposed within hours or days by a few images on a mobile phone. International non-governmental organisations, a free press and mass media have helped to create a climate of public opinion in which private enterprises cannot act with impunity to promote their commercial interests. In the modern economy small, large and multinational firms operate under an extensive framework of national and international law and values, as well as intense public scrutiny. **Chapter 4** discusses more fully these changes and others that shape the social, political and environmental context in which modern companies do business today.

On the other hand, companies have retained that drive to satisfy the consumer's desire for something new, useful and exciting. In the early modern economy, it was products like tea, sugar, chocolate, lightweight clothes, soap and newspapers that belonged to the wealthy few. All these things and more were once the preserve of the rich, but through the innovation of companies in free markets, prices came down, quality improved, and they became much more widely available, just as fridges, TVs, cars, mobile phones and international travel are today. This process of democratising access to elite products and services for ordinary consumers was a key factor in making capitalism more acceptable in society.

In *Empire of Things*,[15] Frank Trentmann argues that the change towards a consumer-centric world began after British success at the battle of Waterloo and the ending of the East India Company's monopoly on trade with India in 1813 when a newly self-confident country began to move towards a free trade policy. He says:

> Free-trade Britain created the world's first consumer-friendly empire. Most immediately, it meant cheaper goods and lower taxes for Britons. Instead of squeezing its people, the British state switched to a path of growth, with low taxes on a rising volume of goods. Consuming more was now public policy.

Capitalism is good at giving ordinary people what they want at a price they can afford. People live only once and they want to enjoy their lives, experiencing as much as possible of what life can offer. This includes the 'stuff' of life: bicycles, mopeds, motor cars, refrigerators, washing machines and, increasingly, the experiences of life, such as taking trips abroad and visits to concerts and the theatre.

What were once luxury goods and special experiences for the rich alone are now being made much more widely available in society and ordinary people can aspire to have them. This is now true on a worldwide basis and poor people in China, India and Africa have access to mobile phones, TVs and radios, which allow them to learn even more about what is available to the masses elsewhere. They then aspire to share in those resources and experiences. The very poor may well need to wait a while to buy what they want, but the dream of being an active consumer of life's pleasures has taken root in the minds of the world's people. It had replaced the utopian communist vision and is the result of the success of millions of private companies providing goods and services to a broad population at a low cost.

Capitalism has retained its amazing ability to change human lives and society through a process of relentless innovation and change. It brings benefits to society, and for consumers in particular. As history shows, however, capitalism also creates negative impacts, in particular on established producer communities and, increasingly, on the natural environment. So humanity's relationship with capitalism truly is a love-hate one.

These issues plague private enterprise today, and the creation of great inequalities of wealth has already been mentioned. In *Capitalism, Socialism and Democracy*,[16] published in the 1940s, Joseph Schumpeter argued that capitalism was endlessly evolving and that it had a crucial element of 'creative destruction' necessarily built into it.

There is then a relentless creativity in the capitalist system that replaces one product with another that is in some way different or better. This can be seen in our transport system, where society moved from pack horse tracks to turnpike roads, to canals, then railroads, then trucks on asphalt roads and aeroplanes today. In writing about one of the most capitalistic countries in the world, the US, Alan Greenspan and Adrian Wooldridge cite examples of 'creative destruction' in *Capitalism in America: A History*,[17] as an important part of social progress, but say why it has been so politically controversial.

> America has been much better than almost every other country at resisting the temptation to interfere with the logic of creative destruction. In most of the world, politicians have made a successful business out of promising the benefits of creative destruction without the costs. Communists have blamed capitalist greed. Populists have blamed them on sinister vested interests. European socialists have taken a more mature approach, admitting that creation and destruction are bound together, but claiming to be able to boost the creative side of creative destruction while eliminating the destructive side through a combination of demand management and wise intervention. The result has usually been disappointing: stagnation, inflation, or some other crisis.

Greenspan and Wooldridge rightly argue that capitalism drove immense social and economic changes in America, but that the country was particularly well endowed with land, raw materials, and its political systems and public values; which allowed the capitalist system to flourish. But like most free-market advocates, they have little to say about the problems it causes. What about those who lost their jobs as a result of these great changes? This is a real issue in societies where populations and labour forces are much more static than in the US, such as in Europe, or in Africa, where a lack of infrastructure and commercial organisation hinder growth.

Greenspan and Wooldridge applaud the fact that the US had an extraordinary degree of social and geographical mobility, which allowed those adversely affected by creative destruction to move to a new frontier and start again. But the fate of producer communities, such as the handloom weavers in India and the coal miners and steel makers in Britain, had their employment seriously damaged by the creative destruction of capitalism. They lost out to international innovation and turned to socialism to remedy their situation. It is no good praising the plethora of consumer opportunities available in society if significant numbers don't have the income to take advantage of them, even as prices come down.

On the other hand, Greenspan and Wooldridge cite the cases of men such as Thomas Edison and Alexander Graham Bell, who each helped found vast new industries, along with Orville and Wilbur Wright, who were the pioneers of the now colossal airline industry. There are many examples in their book of the role of early monopolies and patents as being key to getting ideas turned into profitable products, but what was central to the success of these entrepreneurs was their ability to found companies. This enabled them to raise capital and involve others as shareholders, workers and suppliers, to take these developments forward at scale.

Moore and Lewis's paper has shown that companies, particularly multinational companies, have existed since the start of recorded history. It was not until the middle of the Victorian era, however, that the form of company we know today came in to being. In *Sapiens: A Brief History of Humankind*,[18] Yuval Noah Harari, when discussing the emergence of Peugeot as a major business in France, says:

> Peugeot belongs to a particular genre of legal fictions called 'limited liability companies'. The idea behind such companies is among humanity's most ingenious inventions.

He goes on to say that in early history entrepreneurs who took on debt could be thrown into jail or enslaved if they could not repay it, and people were therefore afraid to start new businesses.

This was why, he explains:

> …people began collectively to imagine the existence of limited liability companies. Such companies were legally independent of the people who set them up, or invested money in them, or managed them. Over the last few centuries such companies have become the main players in the economic arena, and we have grown so used to them that we forget they exist only in our imagination.

It was in Britain in 1844, and then again in 1856, that acts of parliament gave shape and legal form to the modern joint stock limited company in Britain. The great charter companies had relied on the crown or parliament to give them their identity, but from 1856 onwards pretty much anyone could incorporate a limited company. That was a vital innovation at a time when the Industrial Revolution required large amounts of capital to be subscribed to company ventures, because they were often very capital-intensive by their nature. Railway companies, for example, as well as steel and gas works, shipyards and coal mines, all required large amounts of private capital to get going and that could be raised from the public provided the company was a public limited company and met the requirements of the 1856 act.

In addition, these acts of parliament gave companies a distinct 'legal personality', separate from the individuals who were shareholders or managers, and this is a key feature of modern capitalism. Not only has the context in which capitalism operates changed in so many ways, but the idea of the company has changed as well and goes on changing today.

Companies as the Agents of Capitalism

Companies are the vital part of the capitalist system because they are the agents that provide goods and services to the marketplace and make the system work. Entrepreneurs may create whole new industries and new types of goods and services, but it is their companies that deliver them. The companies they create very often outlive the entrepreneur. They have their own constitutions, values and goals to guide and enable those that work in them. Consequently, they can have a very pronounced 'character' of their own; companies are truly distinct 'legal persons' with all the variations of character you can find between different people. The profits made by a business belong to the company as a distinct legal entity, and it is only under strict conditions that limited companies disburse the profits to shareholders.

In the UK today there are several ways that people can do business under the law: they can be sole traders, create a partnership or form a company, which in turn can be either limited or unlimited, as well as private or public. Most countries in the world make provision for the creation of some type of company or private enterprise, but the form the company takes, and its type and structure vary from culture to culture. It is not possible to discuss all these different forms here, but the next chapter sets out the degree to which these private enterprises have come to dominate employment in different countries. What stands out is the degree to which different countries around the world have turned to private enterprises to help take their societies forward in a different way from that which was considered normal even 40 years ago.

But one fact remains the same all around the world: if entrepreneurs, managers and investors wish to act at scale in business, and particularly internationally, they need to form a company to do so. Once formed, it is the company that acts in the marketplace on behalf of the founders, investors (which in western law own the company), managers, employees and others, as a legal personality, just like adult citizens. The company as an organisation has its own rights, responsibilities and legal obligations as it goes about its business in society. Companies are the agents of the capitalist system; they make it work.

In Britain, ever since 1856, the field of company law has been steadily expanding, because once the 1856 act came into being it was possible for any citizen to form a publicly limited company (PLC). The early modern doctrine whereby the state reviewed a company's purpose and gave it a charter 'in the public interest' has been undermined. In post-1856 Britain, anyone who met the conditions laid down in the Companies Act could form a company for purely private purposes. Since 1856, the state in Britain has not seen its role as being one of prescribing the purpose of a private company, merely recognising its existence and regulating the various ways in which it pursues its ends.

The identity of companies in modern society is therefore a relatively new concept, one that is still being fully worked out. There is a presumption, however, that they, like individual citizens, should be left alone, within the law, to get on with doing what they do, and there is no attempt by the state to say what their purpose is or should be.

As social institutions, companies are the small platoons, regiments or even armies in the case of the multinationals that make our economy work. To succeed, they are tightly focused on their freely chosen business mission and must remain successful and disciplined in pursuing it if they are not to fail. Within the basic requirement to make a financial profit to survive, companies, like individuals, have a lot of freedom to make good or bad choices about how to conduct themselves. They do have responsibilities to their stakeholders, especially shareholders as owners, but that is balanced by a good deal of freedom of action, as successive chapters show.

In recent years, the debate about the role of the company in society in western countries has been in broad terms between the American tradition of 'shareholder value' espoused by Milton Friedman and other free-market advocates versus a company's responsibility to its 'stakeholders', that is to say, people who have a stake in the company's activities if not financial shares in it. Typically, stakeholders would include employees, consumers, customers and suppliers who have a real stake in the company's performance, but also others such as communities where they have operations. In some cases, where a company is engaged in major research activities, it can be argued that the science community generally is a stakeholder too.

In recent years, we have added the physical environment to the list of stakeholders too, even though it is not a human entity. Decisions made by the company can have a profound effect on people's lives and the natural environment, as is the case with human stakeholders. Stakeholder theory is today widely recognised as valid, although it is still disputed in public debate by some free-market thinkers, such as Milton Friedman, who claim that championing shareholder primacy and giving them ethical profits should be the guiding purpose of a company.

In the UK, Alan Dignam and John Lowry, in *Company Law*,[19] say:

> Historically, moral philosophy rather than economics has been the dominant influence on the UK debate, centring on moral claims for participation and responsibility towards those affected by the actions of corporations (namely stakeholders), i.e. the employees, customers, creditors, the environment, and the general public.

They acknowledge that companies have an immense amount of power in society and need to be much more broadly accountable for their actions than is suggested in the theory of shareholder supremacy. This book is very much in that British tradition. Having worked in the US for Levi Strauss & Co, which took a stakeholder responsibility view, I have seen at first hand how choosing a stakeholder-based view of a company's responsibilities can bring real benefits to both the company and society.

We must also acknowledge that the role of the shareholder has changed immensely since the days when owner-managers created companies. Today some shares are held for less than a day and most for less than a year. While shareholders technically still own a company, they are generally absent from the decision-making that runs it, where it is the day-to-day decisions of a company's leadership team that express its contract with society. Companies are corporate citizens of society, creating wealth, shaping the lives of millions and impacting the physical environment for good or ill, and the time has come to look again at the social contract we have with them.

The number of private companies has grown immensely in past decades and the next chapter gives some scale to that issue. It also indicates something of the power they have to shape humanity's future as the basis for a discussion of their role in society. Companies are what make capitalism work, and they can do much more to make it work better for society. However, we need to be prepared to accept that they have a positive role to play in society and that with appropriate checks and balances, they can help society move forward in many ways, not just in terms of serving customers and consumers.

CHAPTER 3

Companies in Society Today

Introduction

The previous chapters have shown how communist and socialist governments around the world have backed away from command economies and government ownership, and have given up control of many businesses, particularly the consumer-facing ones. Governments are poor at providing the goods and services that modern, consumer-oriented societies need and want, but for political reasons governments do retain control of many businesses. Over the past few decades, progressively fewer people have worked for government-owned and operated businesses. However, many of the world's major oil companies and airlines, for example, are still government-owned. Nevertheless, the scale of the global change in the expansion of the role of private companies in society cannot be denied.

Chart 1 below shows a selection of countries around the world – led by Cuba, still a socialist country – and the share of the workforce that is employed by the government compared to the percentage working in the private sector, along with some estimates for employment in a small, and often poorly defined non-profit sector. Following Deng's economic revolution, China sits right in the middle of the chart, which shows that many of the world's countries, and a large part of humanity, are now working in market-oriented economies where the government's role as an employer is very limited. There are also millions working in the informal sector, which is not included in the chart because of the difficulties in obtaining reliable statistics on informal sector employment worldwide.

Chart 1 is a best estimate based on data from several sources that do not share common definitions or collect the data in the same way, particularly for the non-profit and informal sectors, where data is especially poor in part because of a lack of a global definition of what types of activities are to be included in it. For example, the chart uses UK data on employment in charities, but many other types of organisation might be included in a more broadly defined non-profit sector if universities and the BBC were included.

It is important to have some sort of estimate to try and create a complete picture of the relative size of the three formal sectors and the informal sector in each society. National governments and international agencies don't seem to collect employment data on the basis of these different sectors, which may imply that they don't see them as being fundamental to how human society is organised and is developing.

These three formal sectors are the three organised, tax paying sectors offering employment in the government and in for-profit and non-profit sector enterprises. We also know that every country, even industrialised ones, has an informal sector and in the less developed countries of Africa, for example, about 85% of the people live and work in the informal sector. Many in this sector are traders and small business people but the number is hard to estimate on a consistent basis. Many people in the informal sector are working in such a way that they could grow their activities to become part of the formal for-profit sector or indeed a formal non-profit sector organisation. These people are very aware, therefore, of the basic rules of business life with respect to maintaining a balance between costs, income and profit.

CHART 1

Estimates of Employment Across Three Formal Sectors

	Government (%)	For profit (%)	Est non-profit (%)
Cuba	85.0	13.0	1–2
Saudi Arabia	68.0	30.0	1–2
Seychelles	43.0	56.0	2–3
Norway	30.0	68.0	2–3
China	22.0	75.0	2–3
UK	17.0	80.0	3*
US	15.0	72.0	12
Brazil	12.0	85.0	2–3
Germany	11.0	82.0	7
Japan	5.9	92.0	5

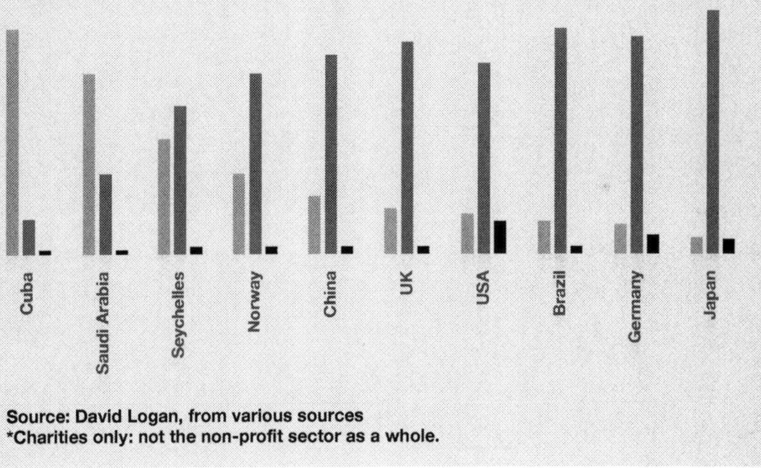

Source: David Logan, from various sources
*Charities only: not the non-profit sector as a whole.

Chart 1 shows that in a communist country such as Cuba, the government still seeks to control 'the means of production' and consequently most people end up working for government-controlled enterprises. In Saudi Arabia, an authoritarian theocracy, the number of government employees is also high, not only because the state controls the huge oil industry (Saudi Aramco), but also because the government wants to retain control of production and work as a means of shaping lives. **Chart 1** also shows that in the liberal, capitalist democracies of Britain and the US, government employment is still substantial in activities such as education, healthcare, the civil service and regulatory agencies, while in Japan and Germany, where postwar reconstruction played a big part in their social organisation, the levels of direct government employment are low.

The chart helps to underline the point of this book, that around the world today far more people work in the private sector than in the state sector, a significant reversal of the postwar trend led by communists and socialists. That change raises tremendous challenges as well as opportunities.

Companies are a Key Part of Our Modern Global Society

In many countries there has been a huge transfer of assets from the governmental sector to the private sector, and on some occasions the non-profit sector. In addition, there has also been an explosion of organic growth in the private sector, and the creation of private companies. **Chapter 1** noted the enormous transfer of publicly owned assets from the British government to the private sector in the 1980s under the leadership of Margaret Thatcher. There has also been a steady growth in the number of private sector companies of all sorts. In the UK there were 3.5m private companies in 2000 and 5.7m in 2018. Many people can see opportunities in private companies, not just economic ones, and they want to engage with them. Private enterprise is no longer the pariah it once was and many people like the freedom and control that running a business brings.

Except for a few countries, such as Cuba and North Korea, what has been happening around the world is the reshaping of human society based on three organised formal sectors. It is not just the for-profit sector that is growing as the state has contracted but also the small, non-profit sector. The size of these three formal sectors varies from country to country, for historical and cultural reasons, but most countries now have them.

Interestingly China, like many other countries, has created a mass of new independent and semi-independent businesses but has not yet created a national enabling legal structure for an independent non-profit sector, one that encompasses the churches, community groups and campaigning organisations developed by ordinary citizens. The Chinese Communist party did create a large number of government-controlled social organisations for youth, churches and trade unions, because it recognised that people need and want such organisations, but the party did not want them to be independent of its control. Even so, independent non-profit organisations have emerged in China, largely because they serve a genuine need among the people, and they consequently exert an influence on society as a whole.

Non-profit organisations, such as churches and religious organisations, are an alternative centre of ideas to that of the state, and authoritarian rulers don't like them for that reason. The communists are very aware that the non-profit Catholic church in Poland and the Lutheran church in East Germany played important roles in undermining the rule of the party in those countries. After membership of the Communist party in China, the followers of Falun Gong, the Christian churches and Islam are some of the most organised groups in the country. For that reason, and also because of their different world view, these non-profits are treated with suspicion by the government, particularly if they have international connections.

Chart 2 summarises the pattern of the three formal sectors of modern society. It is a pattern that seems to be emerging organically around the world, because it serves people's different needs and wants. It is one where the three formal sectors of society (the governmental, the private for-profit and the non-profit sectors) interact with one another alongside a sizeable informal sector where the lives of everyday people and their families are lived. The informal sector is huge and is based on people doing things for each other on a voluntary basis, or for small cash payments that are not regulated or taxed as the other formal sectors are.

CHART 2
The Three Formal Sectors of a Global Society

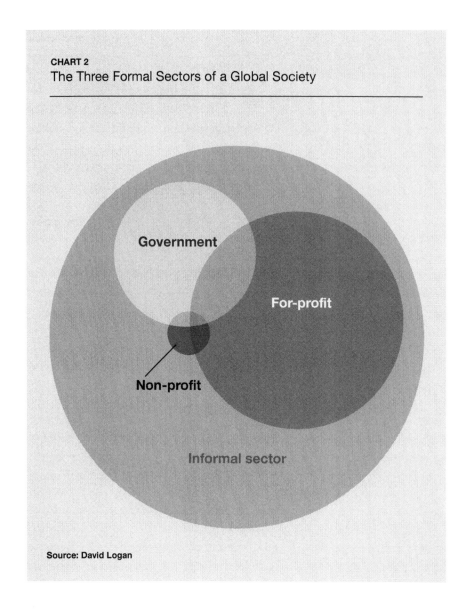

Source: David Logan

Chart 2 represents a view of how global society is developing now that the scale of state enterprise has been limited in most countries. In the UK, it is important to note that Mrs Thatcher not only transferred assets from the governmental sector to the private sector, but also sold some local government housing, for example, directly to sitting tenants in the informal sector or transferred them to non-profit housing associations. To shrink the state, Conservative politicians were only too happy to see the non-profit sector grow as well as the for-profit sector. The traditional communist left was of course opposed to either sector having a wider role in society.

Chart 2 does show these three formal sectors overlapping in their activities, and that is what is demanded by the issues facing humanity today. There are often contacts between two or sometimes all three sectors to address an issue, but there are huge impediments to a long-term, systematic engagement to an extent that works for the public good. A key one is that private companies don't necessarily see it as their role to contribute significantly to solving society's problems; they see their role as one of serving customers and consumers while giving their shareholders a 'good return' on their investment.

Companies see their role primarily as interacting with the informal sector through the marketplace, rather than helping shoulder the wider burdens of society, which they leave to the state and the non-profit sector. Both these sectors see their role as explicitly serving the people through their activities, whereas companies are first and foremost seen as serving private profit.

To give more substance to the concept embodied in **Chart 2**, it is worth seeing how it plays out in the single country example of the UK, where employment data by sector is available on a common basis. A different view of the relationship between the three formal sectors in the UK is presented in **Chart 3**, where the enormous role of private companies in employment is obvious; private companies of various sorts dominate the working lives of the people of Britain. The figure for the non-profit sector is for charities only, as the definition in UK government figures is a narrow one. Charities constitute only one part of the wider non-profit sector. In addition, it is hard to get an accurate figure for the number of jobs that exist in the informal sector, so the figure of 2m is a best estimate. However, **Chart 3** makes the substantial point that it is private sector employment that dominates the working lives of ordinary Britons.

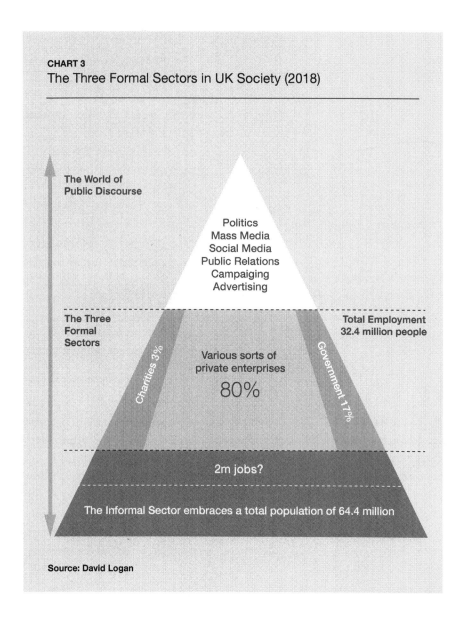

CHART 3

The Three Formal Sectors in UK Society (2018)

The World of
Public Discourse

Politics
Mass Media
Social Media
Public Relations
Campaiging
Advertising

The Three
Formal
Sectors

Total Employment
32.4 million people

Charities 3%

Various sorts of
private enterprises

80%

Government 17%

2m jobs?

The Informal Sector embraces a total population of 64.4 million

Source: David Logan

Chart 3 also identifies the 'world of public discourse' as the public arena in which society's issues get thrashed out. All three of the formal sectors and the informal sector feed into this public discourse, but it has a life of its own, as it is often driven by the mass media, and by today's social media at the disposal of individual communicators of all sorts. It is out of this wide-ranging public debate that legislation may arise to initiate changes and social trends of all sorts are developed. It was noted in **Chapter 1** that the world of public discourse can be strongly influenced by cultural commentators who have never worked for a private company, never would, and are deeply suspicious of the profit motive. There is a whole world of cultural opinion-formers who don't seek to engage in any depth with what companies do and how they work; at best they are seen as a necessary evil.

It is important to recognise that around the world our society is maintained, and our civilisation primarily built, by everyday work. Much of this we take for granted and we barely recognised its importance until the Covid-19 crisis struck in 2020; people saw the tremendous impact of the virus on the 'economy' of closing down so many businesses. It became painfully obvious that the economy was not an abstract thing but an aggregation of the activities of hundreds of thousands of businesses and non-profit organisations. It is easy to forget that nothing is produced, and no service is offered by any of the three formal sectors unless it is to be used or otherwise consumed by the people. It is the purposeful activities of the three organised sectors that form a critical foundation for whatever is said and done in the world of public discourse.

Companies are their own worst enemies in this arena. They try to influence the realm of public discourse through advertising, public relations and, less obviously, political lobbying. As a rule, they don't like to be dragged into wider public debates about issues, and they like to keep a low profile and get on with doing business. Their links with the other two formal sectors are often limited to lobbying the government for commercial advantage, while making charitable donations and other community contributions to the non-profit sector.

There are real issues about how companies are portrayed in public discourse. Often the only publication they produce about their activities is a financial report aimed at shareholders and focused on financial performance. These reports are not a lot of help in explaining their contribution to society. For this we must thank the growth in the number of corporate social responsibility (CSR) and sustainability reports in recent years, which have helped put useful data into the public domain and explain the dilemmas companies face, so that society can see the wider contributions that they make.

The Rise of the For-Profit Sector

The growth, scale and structure of the for-profit sector around the world is much better recorded than that of the non-profit sector. Since the collapse of communism around the world, there has been a huge surge in the number of companies being created each year, and today it is estimated that there are over 190m private companies in the world. Also, with the growth in stock markets around the world, there has been a rapid growth in the number of large, listed companies. In 2019, the OECD published a report[20] in which it said:

> At the end of 2017, there were approximately 41,000 listed companies in the world. Their combined market value was about USD 84 trillion, which is equivalent to global GDP.

In more than 8% of these publicly listed companies, the governments of countries such as China own more than 50% of the shares in them. The governments of Saudi Arabia and Norway are also major corporate shareholders, and overall governments own about 14% of the stock value of these listed companies. However, 41% of global market capitalisation is owned by institutional investors, such as mutual funds, pension funds and insurance companies, while about 18% of stocks combined are held by private corporations, including holding companies, and individuals or families. These categories of owner are what Marx saw as the traditional 'rentier' capitalist class of people who lived on profits from investments.

These figures are indicative of the surge in growth of the worldwide for-profit sector and the major role it is beginning to play in our global civilisation. To better understand how companies operate in society, it is worth looking in detail at the UK, which is a good example of how companies in many industrialised countries are organised. **Chart 4** breaks down the private sector into its various types of companies. Overall, the number of businesses of all types has grown by about 60% since 2000, when there were 3.5m recorded businesses.

The UK Office for National Statistics tells us that about 32.5 million UK citizens were employed in formal sector jobs in 2018, and as **Chart 3** showed, just over 27 million or about 80% were employed in for-profit sector companies. Although most of them work in small and medium-sized companies, **Chart 4** shows that just over 7,500 large companies employ 10 million people. These businesses with more than 250 employees represent about 0.1 per cent of all formally constituted companies but are responsible for about half of the turnover (revenue) of the sector. Some are in private family companies, others are large, publicly listed companies, and clearly their day-to-day impact on society is immense.

Consequently, to make significant changes to the economic, social and environmental issues in which companies are involved, we need to change the policies and practices of only 7,500 large companies. Converting 7,500 companies to sound social and environmental practices may well be a lot easier than converting a whole national population of around 60 million. If the 35,000 or so businesses with between 50 and 249 employees are added to the total, approximately two-thirds of the for-profit sector's turnover is covered and a great deal of change may be effected.

CHART 4

Companies in the UK For-Profit Sector (2018)

Size of business by number of employees	Number of companies	Number of employees (1,000s)	% of sector turnover
Totals*	*5,667,510	27,027	100
Small and Medium 0–249	5,660,000	16,284	52
Large 250+	7,510	10,743	48

*Includes 4.2m businesses, with no employees, but includes sole proprietorships and partnerships with only the self-employed owner manager and companies with a single employee, who are assumed to be a director.

Source: Department For Business, Energy and Industrial Strategy: Statistical Release October 2018

There are issues where it is important to change the values, ideas and practices of the whole population but there are also many issues where businesses can initiate change and confront an issue before we need to change the behaviour of the whole population. Eliminating unnecessary packaging and getting rid of unrecyclable packaging is a good example, but the population as a whole still needs to take responsibility for recycling. The various campaigns to get food companies to reduce the fat and salt in their products are further examples of a pre-emptive move by businesses to address the social problems of obesity and diabetes. Pre-emptive action by companies can do much to address important economic, social and environmental issues.

Furthermore, at the level of industrial sectors, it is possible for companies in whole industries to come together to make changes that reduce their negative impacts and confront economic, social and environmental problems. The hotel industry, for example, has voluntarily developed a green hotels policy that member companies can use to reduce their environmental impacts. Only 10 to 12 or so companies need to be involved to change the policies and practices of the modern internet-based companies of Silicon Valley, such as Facebook, Twitter and Apple. Together they have leadership teams of about 400 to 500 people who have the power to radically change the way their companies work and impact society all around the world.

Private companies provide us with all manner of goods and services, and they have an immense impact on our lives through the products and services they offer, such as our food, clothes, houses, furniture, drugs, cars and endless electrical gadgets, not to mention the electricity to drive them, and music, entertainment, foreign travel and financial services. Consequently, the idea that companies are 'citizens' of society and have a part to play in addressing its economic, social and environmental concerns must be part of our thinking, nationally and globally. We cannot solve many of our most pressing problems without engaging the for-profit sector; it is just too big and powerful to be ignored.

Problems with Capitalism Remain

However, companies do not sit comfortably as part of modern society. A major reason why they are not readily seen as being citizens of society is in the name of the sector. It is called the 'for-profit sector'; the very notion of profit is viewed with suspicion by many in society. Profit is still seen as a purely private benefit whereas the other two formal sectors are at least seen as working to benefit society as a whole. The governmental sector is supposed, in principle, to serve the people; similarly, the growing non-profit sector serves the people with a passion that comes from strong voluntary commitment.

The for-profit sector, on the other hand, is seen as committed to making profit for private benefit and what is there to like about that? Companies are seen as being about the self-interest of the owners and shareholders, not the public good. Given this, can humanity really expect much in the way of promoting public good from such self-interested entities? The idea of 'profit' as a concept remains controversial. It is discussed below with four other issues that mark out the for-profit sector as being different from the other two formal sectors, illustrating the difficulty people find in seeing the for-profit sector as a force for the common good.

However, before looking at why it is difficult to fit businesses and companies into partnership with the other two formal sectors in promoting public good, it is worth considering that running a business is not solely the prerogative of the for-profit sector. The other two formal sectors run businesses too. The profits that businesses make can be very attractive to the other two formal sectors so long as they control the profits or 'surpluses' and plough them back into their other activities. It is worth remembering that governments own oil and airline companies, the largest cigarette business in the world is owned by the Chinese government, and governments run alcoholic drinks businesses and gambling firms. Despite huge divestments of state businesses all around the world, governments still own and run business enterprises of all sorts.

The non-profit sector is also active in setting up businesses and running them to make a profit, or surplus, for the benefit of their organisation and its beneficiaries. For example, about 40% of Oxfam's annual income came from trading activities in 2018 and many charitable organisations also engage in gambling by running lotteries, as does the British government. Furthermore, many charities spend time and money helping people in the developing world set up small businesses as a means of generating an income for themselves and their families. These businesses are small, so not open to the same degree of suspicion as large companies, but they do trade in the marketplace and use the same fundamental rules that all businesses must observe to survive, such as meeting consumer needs and making a profit.

There are more cross-connections between the formal sectors in terms of business activities than first meets the eye. These issues need to be addressed because they contribute to the continuing hostility toward private companies, which can easily be portrayed as inherently antisocial, serving only private interests. In turn, this hostility contributes to a defensive mindset in companies that don't seek a wider, more positive role in society. Also, there is a lack of awareness in society itself, as to how to engage companies in problem-solving and partnerships.

Additionally, we must recognise that the self-interest of for-profit companies is not all bad. Long ago Adam Smith showed how the self-interest of private companies and entrepreneurs in providing goods and services to society can also serve the public good. As China has shown, growing a 'self-interested' private sector can create broader benefits for society, such as creating new jobs and wealth. However, allowing a for-profit sector to flourish does raise other issues about the wider impact of the capitalist system and the behaviour of the companies that make it up.

So, five general questions about the nature of capitalism and a company's role in society are addressed below, starting with the problem of profit, because they remain very much part of people's thinking about the capitalist system. There are many more questions that bear consideration, such as the external diseconomies that companies can create, the relentless use of natural resources and the promotion of consumerism, but some issues, such as international tax policy and executive pay, are within the competence of companies to deal with themselves. However, until we are clear about some key perceptions of the capitalist system, it is going to be difficult to get business into partnership with the other two formal sectors to promote the public good.

1. The Problem of Profit

The whole concept of 'profit' itself is generally viewed with suspicion in society and it is widely assumed that capitalism is a zero-sum game where one person's profit is another person's loss. The vision of a capitalist as a rich, uncaring individual who seeks to profit as much as possible from exploiting other people at work or in the marketplace is still alive in cultures around the world. This persists even though publicly owned businesses are much more likely to be using their profits to support the savings and pension funds of teachers, nurses and ordinary people. In 2014, only about 12% of the shares on the London stock market were owned by individuals; institutional shareholders predominate, often working on behalf of millions of ordinary people.

Furthermore, when economists talk about the workings of the marketplace, they do so by making key assumptions, such as the laws of supply and demand determining prices, and that the primary purpose of a company is to maximise profits. This latter assumption is a widely held belief across a spectrum of economic thinkers, from Karl Marx to Milton Friedman, and seems to be a staple idea in university teaching today. If this idea were true, and the sole purpose of a company were to maximise profits, then there would little or no room for a discussion about stakeholder interests, corporate responsibility and good corporate citizenship.

There is plenty of scope for maximising profit in the for-profit sector and it would be stupid to deny that this happens. However, central to understanding what large companies broadly think about their role in society, it is important to know what they think of profit maximisation as the main aim of business.

What companies say to their shareholders about profit-making is therefore a critical consideration, and very few listed companies say to shareholders that their role is to maximise profits. This is because in reality companies tend to take a long-term view of their future and know that if they want regular, repeat business, they must take stakeholders' and society's concerns into account, along with other business considerations. Short-term maximising does not support long-term company success.

In *The Mission Statement Book*,[21] published in the 1990s, there is a collection of 301 corporate mission statements issued mainly by listed companies. These mission statements are the prospectuses that companies present to potential shareholders and to society, and they very often define the purpose of the company.

In the book, only a small number said they would maximise profits as part of their commitment to shareholders. They were much more inclined to say that they would give a "fair return" or a *"good return"* to shareholders. To give shareholders a more precise statement of intentions, Johnson Controls Inc is quoted as saying, "We will exceed the after-tax, median return on shareholders' equity of the Standard & Poor's Industrials." Many companies tell shareholders that they will give them a return that is benchmarked in terms of the value growth of shares and their dividend yield, against a specified group of peers and competitors. What they don't say is, "We will maximise your investment."

Box 1 in **Chapter 5** quotes in full the 'credo' or mission statement for the Johnson & Johnson Company, and it says of its commitment to shareholders, that it will give them a "sound profit", not a maximum one. Contrary to popular opinion, most large, publicly listed companies do not seek to maximise profits. They are long-term profit optimisers that seek to take in to account the interests of stakeholders and the wider society in their operations. They will seek to give shareholders a "good" return but not at the expense of their longer-term operating needs and stakeholder relationships.

What happens in practice in most companies is that owners and managers balance their commitments to stakeholders and society in such a way that the company survives from year to year. In some years, the shareholder takes the hit and gets little or no dividend; in other years the employees may take the hit as the company downsizes and cuts jobs; or customers and consumers may see price rises and suppliers may lose contracts while communities see local plants close. Companies do have to make a profit to survive in the commercial game, but to suggest that they exist only to maximise profits is to seriously misunderstand what drives them; it is a lazy assumption that limits the discussion of their role in society.

2. The Size and Power of Companies

Another reason why some people feel companies should not have a wider role in working with the other two sectors is that some companies are just too big and powerful. Multinational companies in particular can be very big, much bigger than many governments, and consequently people don't trust them not to promote their self-interest with the government or interfere in the realm of public discourse.

Walmart, a US retailer, is the largest listed company quoted in the Fortune Global 500. In 2018, it had sales of just over $500bn and 2.3 million direct employees, with many millions more working in its huge and diverse supply chain around the world. If sales were compared to GDP, Walmart would be similar in size to Nigeria (GDP $496.12bn) and Iran (GDP $495.59bn), but that is not an accurate comparison, although it is often made. The real comparator of a country's GDP is the cash 'value added' companies produce each year. Simply stated, that is the money left in the business after all supplier costs have been subtracted but few companies produce that figure.

One company that does so regularly is Unilever (167th in the 2019 Fortune Global 500). In 2018 it had sales of approximately €51bn and spent €34bn on suppliers, leaving a cash value added figure for the company of approximately €17bn; that means it is larger in cash terms than Jamaica, which has a GDP of $15.7bn. In addition, Unilever has about 155,000 direct employees worldwide, but creates many more jobs in its extensive supply chain around the world. Unilever estimates that one or more of its products are consumed by up to 2.5 billion people every day. So, Unilever is a powerful force for shaping life on the planet.

In a study published jointly with Oxfam[22] in 2005 looking at the social and economic impact of Unilever in one country, Indonesia, it was suggested that around 3,400 jobs in the company, and the 3,600 full-time jobs of contract workers and 'co-packer' suppliers working solely for the company, supported the full-time job equivalent of an estimated 105,000 jobs in the supply chain and 188,000 jobs in distribution and retail. Thus, the activity of the company had a much wider impact on society through job creation, as well as through its sale of products, such as soap, shampoo and foodstuffs, not to mention the taxes it paid and the innovation it fostered.

Consequently, governments and international trade agencies may well be more inclined to listen to large companies such as Unilever than to small campaigning groups. Their huge size, coupled with the number of people involved in their activities, demands attention. A company's self-interest is not just about that of shareholders but also of employees, customers, consumers, and communities. As long as companies are lobbying for their interests in an ethical and transparent way, they are entitled to do so. They should not, of course, be operating behind closed doors and paying bribes as part of expressing their self-interest, which would be the antithesis of socially responsible behaviour. Large companies will stand up for their own self-interest; what else should we expect? But the regulators will always have the last say.

3. Companies Make Some People Very Rich

Capitalism suits some people very well; they thrive in the system, but not everybody does. There are millions of businesses in Britain and the directors and managers of these companies, if not the ordinary employees, may well be on the route to great wealth. As the number of private businesses has risen around the world, there has been a rise in economic inequality. As a non-profit that combines projects giving direct service and campaigning, Oxfam recognises that progress has been made in reducing poverty, but it campaigns hard against economic inequality, and published a report on the issue, *Even It Up: Time to End Extreme Inequality*.[23] Oxfam's website says:

> In 2013, seven out of 10 people lived in countries where economic inequality was worse than 30 years ago, and in 2014 Oxfam calculated that just 85 people owned as much as the poorest half of humanity.

There can be no doubt that economic inequality has grown rapidly with the re-emergence of a global private sector, but what can be done about it? Most of the wealth today comes to people through successful companies and that is a major source of suspicion of the private sector. Those who are very wealthy may well have government bonds, properties and gold, but it is their ownership of shares in private companies that is the real source of their wealth.

In *The Price of Inequality*,[24] Joseph E Stiglitz addresses the issue of economic inequality in respect of the US. One of his conclusions is the idea that in a true community economic inequality is not inevitable to the degree he believes the US is currently experiencing it. He introduces the powerful idea that 'self-interest', which is seen as the heart of capitalism, has another aspect of some importance where inequality is concerned:

> Alexis de Tocqueville once described what he saw as a chief element of the peculiar genius of American society, something he called "self-interest properly understood". The last two words were key. Everyone possesses self-interest in a narrow sense: I want what is good for me right now! Self-interest "properly understood" is different. It means appreciating that paying attention to everyone else's self-interest – in other words, to the common welfare – is in fact a precondition for one's own ultimate well-being.

Like a lot of people on the left of the debate about inequality, Stiglitz essentially sees the solution to economic inequality lying in political action and increased taxes on the rich, some of which may well be necessary in respect of this issue. However, by quoting Alexis de Tocqueville, he has opened the door to companies and wealthy individuals acting voluntarily to address the issue. He may well be right about the need for legislation and taxes, but he recognises that companies and the people that own shares in them also have the freedom to choose how they behave in respect of the distribution of the wealth that companies create.

Self-interest properly understood means companies thinking about everyone in society who is impacted by their business activities and beyond. Not everyone does well in the capitalist system and the welfare states that have developed in many countries are a sign that the needs of those who don't flourish in a free market environment also have to be catered for if a capitalist society is to be allowed to continue. If there is one thing we should have learned from history it is that capitalism cannot be allowed to benefit the rich alone.

Furthermore, around the world there is great concern about the ability of wealthy individuals to use their influence on governments and the whole democratic process. Crony capitalism is a worry for many societies, not only in Russia, as the expansion of the for-profit sector around the world has led not only to serious economic inequalities but also to concentrations of political power in some societies. This is another significant problem for advocates of free-market economic policies.

However, some of the very wealthy are also concerned about these problems, as *The Times* reported in January 2020,[25] when it published a story about billionaires and millionaires asking to pay more tax:

More than 120 wealthy celebrities and business people urged their peers to step up and call for tax increases across the world "before it is too late".

Identifying themselves as "members of the most privileged class of human beings ever to walk the Earth", they claimed that tensions caused by economic disparities were at crisis level, resulting in erosion of trust within societies, increased resentment and the undermining of basic social cohesion.

This basic pattern of inequality is not going to change in the short term and fundamentally is up to governments to counterbalance this development. Only governments can act at scale to set national tax laws and create international treaties to regulate the income and wealth of all the rich. Governments set the rules for greater economic equality, and campaigning groups in the non-profit sector will be there to urge them on. In the meantime, the idea of 'self-interest properly understood' will be a key driver of the philanthropy of many rich people who understand it, including Bill and Melinda Gates.

What this book is trying to explore is what companies might do, as distinct corporate citizens, to address inequality as a social issue. It is important not to stereotype all wealthy people and all companies as the enemies of economic justice. It is companies that set pay rates for top executives and ordinary workers. They have the power to spread the benefits of shareholding much more widely; they can change policies about the use of offshore tax havens to shelter profits; and they can provide benefits and opportunities to ordinary workers that can do much to improve their lives.

4. Relentless Innovation Remains Integral to Capitalism

Joseph Schumpeter was right to argue that the 'creative destruction' of capitalism drives economic processes in a market-based society; the constant creation of new goods and services and the abandonment of the old is an integral part of the capitalist system. It forces change, and many don't like that. Capitalism, led by the innovation of individuals and companies, is constantly confronting society with new opportunities and challenges. For example, if a company downsizes or moves production offshore, employees, suppliers and communities can suffer major losses of employment, and in the short term at least, their wellbeing is damaged by the decision.

The problems that this increasingly rapid form of change can create are of deep concern to many, and it is obvious that not all stakeholders share equally in the burdens imposed by such company decisions. Employees have much more at stake than investors, and even consumers. Like shareholders, consumers have benefited from globalisation (buying garments, smartphones and holidays), but workers in many industries have seen their wages stagnate and manufacturing jobs go overseas. Furthermore, suppliers of manufactured and even agricultural goods now face competition from producers in former communist and socialist countries that were not previously part of the global economy.

Precisely because companies have taken advantage of the opportunities that globalisation has brought, they are more likely to be seen by many, particularly workers in traditional industries, as the cause of society's problems. Consequently, writers such as Joseph Stiglitz, campaigning non-profit organisations, and politicians (on the left and the right) have attacked globalisation and the companies that have led the process, with little thought going into how companies might mitigate the change process for those affected.

When I worked for Levi Strauss & Co, the company faced tremendous competitive pressure from companies sourcing jeans and other garments from overseas and had to start closing plants. But as it did so, the company developed programmes to help workers and communities with training and new employment initiatives that helped ease the transition process. Levi Strauss was just one of a number of companies that took these steps. In the 1980s in the UK a business-led non-profit organisation, Business in the Community, mobilised many businesses to help with job creation and education for workers and young people who were faced with huge economic disruption caused by industrial restructuring and globalisation. Today, challenges such as the impact of artificial intelligence on traditional jobs such as truck driving can in part be addressed by the companies taking action to compensate for job losses and help workers make the transition to new forms of employment.

5. The Real Economy and High Finance

When discussing capitalism, the world of 'high finance' is seen as being vital to the working of the system. To a large extent this is true, and it is this world of high finance and investment banking that is particularly unpopular in society. After all, the financial crisis of 2008–09, which led to huge disruption in the economy, was almost wholly created by the world of banks and investment houses operating primarily in the bond market, not the stock market. Nevertheless, throughout history stock markets have played a vital role in helping companies to raise the capital to invest and innovate and while they are in decline today (the UK stock market had 12,400 listed companies in 2000, but there are only about 5,700 today and the US stock markets have contracted similarly), they remain an important part of the capitalist system.

In many ways the 2008–09 financial crisis was the high-tide mark of the Thatcher and Reagan years of deregulation and reliance on free markets. Only governments' enormous intervention in the financial markets stabilised the economy, but even so, many countries faced lengthy periods of austerity in government spending, which proved very unpopular. The world of high finance is pretty much a law unto itself and this book has little to say about its role in the capitalist system. The reader is better advised to turn to the books of Michael Lewis for insights as to how it works and what might be changed about it. There is much discussion about regulating the world of high finance: for example, whether a 'Tobin' tax on share trading is a good idea.

However, the global financial system is still largely parasitic on the activities of the many private companies that make up the day-to-day reality of the capitalist system. Financiers make money in many ways such as currency trading, but investments in companies producing goods and services for consumption are central to what they do. These companies live and work in the 'real economy', which trades in the marketplace. They constitute most of the companies in the capitalist system; they are the companies where ordinary people work, shop and invest. They are the frontline of economic, social and environmental impact on the world.

Companies Have the Freedom to Choose

The overall impact of the capitalist system will continue to be debated with passion, and despite the issues touched on above, most of the world's companies will go on doing business every day. They will be serving customers and consumers, employing millions and developing supply chains that touch communities everywhere around the world. Despite the constraints of the market, and the need to make a profit and satisfy shareholders with dividends, leaders of these companies still have the freedom to choose how they behave in respect of many vital issues in society.

Companies and their executives will still be criticised for a wide range of issues beyond those mentioned above, such as monopoly power, burdening society with external diseconomies, promoting excessive consumption, unfair tax policy, excessive executive pay, a lack of gender equality in management, human rights in the supply chain, and a whole range of negative environmental impacts. However, one thing remains clear: despite the overarching nature of the capitalist system, and within the existing framework of law, companies can still act decisively on many issues and in doing so influence the form of capitalism generally.

In the past, to answer Marxist challenges about who owns the business assets and gets the profits, some company founders and owners chose to give their businesses to their workers. The creation of the John Lewis Partnership and the Scott Bader Commonwealth are good examples and there are about 400 employee-owned businesses of various sizes in the UK. The formation of employee and consumer co-operatives are another way of answering Marxist questions of who get the profits and takes the value of workers' labour. Substantial financial mutual and building societies have been developed and social enterprises have grown rapidly in recent years. There are now 2,600 members of Social Enterprise UK and these businesses have chosen to develop first and foremost around social and environmental missions, returning profits made to their primary purpose, not to owners and shareholders.

About 5,000 companies worldwide have chosen to follow the B Corporation model and have set out to build into the constitution of the company a commitment to economic, social and environmental responsibility. It is possible to get companies to voluntarily commit to responsible behaviour within the existing capitalist framework of ideas and law. But even so, these initiatives are relatively small compared with the mass of ordinary companies that exist, and it is those companies that **Chapter 5** addresses.

Companies are the most important institutions in the free-market system and we must learn to bring them much more effectively into the fight to address the great range of problems that humanity faces. They are central to our civilisation's development and survivability but as they have grown in size and importance in the post-communist world, so have independent non-profit organisations, and it is important to know how they too fit into the pattern of social institutions developing organically around the world. In Britain, the early growth of the for-profit sector was the primary stimulus for the development of the English-speaking world's first campaigning non-profit organisation.

The Rise of the Non-Profit Sector

As the early modern economy developed in Britain, merchants were trading in agricultural products such as sugar, tobacco and cotton cloth, which were produced by slave labour. Enslaved Africans imported into the Caribbean, North America and Latin America were crucial to the colonial economies of the time and the trade in human lives was itself very profitable. It was widely accepted commercial activity, and few gave it a second thought. However, it was this commercial activity that prompted the first example of a campaigning non-profit organisation in the English-speaking world, and as modern capitalism grew, so did many campaigning non-profit organisations.

The rise of opposition to the Atlantic slave trade and African slavery is described by Adam Hochschild in his insightful book, *Bury The Chains; the British Struggle to Abolish Slavery*.[26] He shows how a group of concerned citizens came together in May 1787 to form a committee to abolish the slave trade. It was an international trade or business, which supported diverse commercial activities, including meeting the rapidly growing consumer demand for cheap sugar and other tropical goods.

Hochschild says of this independent committee of ordinary citizens:

> They had to ignite their crusade in a country where the great
> majority of people, from farmhands to bishops, accepted slavery
> as completely normal. It was also a country where profits from
> West Indian plantations gave a large boost to the economy, where
> customs duties on slave-grown sugar were an important source
> of government revenue, and where the livelihoods of tens of
> thousands of seamen, merchants and ship builders depended on
> the slave trade... How even to begin the massive job of changing
> public opinion? Furthermore, nineteen out of twenty Englishmen,
> and all English women, were not even allowed to vote. Without
> this basic right themselves, could they be roused to care about the
> rights of other people, of a different skin colour, an ocean away?
>
> In all human experience, there was no precedent for such a
> campaign.

Over the next two decades, the campaign committee went on to develop
all the techniques of campaigning and communication that such groups
use today: they endorsed 'slave-free' sugar (Fairtrade is not new), they sent
endless petitions to parliament, they lobbied individual MPs, and their
wives used eye-catching visual images of slave ships, got critical reports
in the newspapers, and even organised direct mail fundraising. Through
their passion for their cause, they changed the moral climate of the whole
country and brought down the vast commercial interests supporting
slavery. These interests fought them at every turn, but by 1806 the British
government passed laws to abolish the slave trade. This was the first
example of the power of campaigning non-profit organisations to change
society, and by their actions they showed that they could hold businesses
and the government to account.

So as modern commerce and society developed, the non-profit sector
developed with it. Campaigning and providing services, non-profit
organisations began to be an organic part of the shape of modern society.
Along with developments in the free press, the law and political democracy,
independent non-profit organisations became an integral part of a free-
market society, and they have played a critical role up to now. They can
challenge the behaviour of businesses and the government and compensate

for their lack of engagement with issues by providing goods and services that the other two formal sectors fail to do.

It is worth quoting the case of the campaign against the slave trade at length, because the commercial decisions that led to it still shape our world today; as the Black Lives Matter campaign in 2020 has once again brought to the fore. The racial discrimination and racism that has come from slavery still haunt our world today and bring suffering in the US and beyond, to many people of African descent.

Sir David Attenborough recently cited the British campaign against the slave trade in a TV interview when discussing the problem of climate change. He argued that a complete change in society's attitude to carbon generation was urgently needed, despite the enormous economic and other benefits that are still accruing from fossil fuels. He argued that it was possible, by creative campaigning, to get people to think very differently about their world and positively want to change it, as they did when the slave trade was abolished.

Campaigning non-profit organisations have a huge role to play in society, despite their relatively small size; they can be key in changing the way people think about life. That in turn feeds through to what companies and indeed governments can and cannot do. For it was not only business that was the focus of this early campaigning activity at around the time that the slave trade was abolished in 1806: Elizabeth Fry and others were beginning to demand that the British government reform conditions in prisons and convict transportation, which they were ultimately obliged to do.

The Non-Profit Sector Today

As societies change around the world, the non-profit sector is growing because it helps meet people's unmet needs in society. However, defining the non-profit sector as a group of institutions is not easy in a global context. It includes charities, non-governmental organisations (NGOs), citizen action groups, voluntary organisations, trade unions, charitable foundations and independent bodies such as universities and the BBC. There are many names used for it, including 'the independent sector', 'the voluntary or charity sector', in French 'l'économie sociale', the 'tax-exempt sector, and today, a very widely used name is 'civil society'.

This is the term used by Civicus, which was founded in 1993 and acts as a sort of international trade association for a wide range of voluntary organisations that make up the non-profit sector. What all the organisations that it represents have in common is that they are not part of the government and they do not make or distribute profits to owners and shareholders (although some do create 'surpluses' from their activities).

In their pioneering study, *Defining the Nonprofit Sector; a cross-national analysis*,[27] Lester M Salamon and Helmut K Anheier say:

> Even non-profit sector, the term we will generally use here, is not without problems. This term emphasizes the fact that these organizations do not exist primarily to generate profits for their owners. But these organizations sometimes do earn profits, i.e., they generate more revenues than they spend in a given year.

In the context of this book, the term 'non-profit' does nicely differentiate the sector from the for-profit sector and that is one good reason to follow Salamon and Anheier and use their definition. Another is that they, like Civicus, include a broad range of organisations in their definition, not just charities. Non-profit organisations are characteristically independent of the state and serve society in education, including universities, healthcare, social services, self-help and charitable activities; as well as in communications organisations such as the BBC and the US Public Broadcasting Service. As organisations, they are defined first and foremost by their public service mission, and should their income from donations, trading activities and more exceed their spending in a given year, they plough it back into the public service works of the organisation.

The sector embodies the power of ordinary citizens when they act to create organisations to take altruistic action on the economic, social and environmental issues that concern them. Non-profit organisations can be created by individuals and groups just as private companies are, but they don't have private purposes: they serve a defined public good. They have overtly public purposes, and unless they can demonstrate this purpose, they do not qualify for the status of a charity and receive the corresponding tax breaks, but they can be part of the wider non-profit sector.

Most non-profit organisations are in fact service providers and may or may not have charitable status. They are caring for people's needs in many ways and they grow out of people's experience of the world and the desire of the organisation's founders to meet the many needs often unmet or poorly met by the other two formal sectors. There are many needs that the state has not recognised and the for-profit sector does not cater for; or if it does, at a price ordinary people cannot afford to pay, such as long-term care for elderly people.

In the UK, a good modern example of a creative non-profit organisation in the caring world would be that of Dr Cicely Saunders, who, from her personal experience was inspired to create the independent hospice network. When she discovered that neither the existing charitable organisations nor the state properly catered for the needs of people at the end of their lives, she launched her own response to this problem with charitable finance, and so created the first modern hospice. It gave care along lines that she had identified as being necessary and was a big improvement on what others did.

Out of that first example, a worldwide movement has grown up, based on her philosophy of hospice practice and supported by voluntary public subscriptions. While the hospice movement is primarily providing a direct service to people in society, its practical work has, through example, also changed public attitudes and governmental policy towards this major issue.

However, the non-profit sector also is home to specialist campaigning organisations. Their service to society is first and foremost to operate in the world of public discourse and to push for reform in respect of a wide range of issues. Some organisations, for example in the field of family violence, do both, providing refuges for battered women while also campaigning for the reform of relevant laws, public policy and social attitudes. Other organisations, such as Amnesty International, are purely campaigning organisations whose work is vitally important as an extension of democracy and the parliamentary process. They allow ordinary citizens to voice concerns about issues where they feel changes are necessary and to confront governments and companies they see as acting badly.

At their best, campaigning non-profit organisations can change public policy and right wrongs, as well as ensuring services to underserved populations.

They do this by engaging in the world of public discourse as shown in **Chart 3**. As Salamon and Anheier show, campaigning organisations are a growing force around the world as they help mobilise people to confront various economic, social and environmental issues in societies. Many recent campaigns by non-profit organisations – on fair pay, child labour in agriculture and factories, gender equality in the workplace, and reducing carbon and water usage – all show how influential non-profit organisations of various sorts can be in changing company behaviour. Consequently, companies need to listen to them, learn from them and partner with them on issues of importance that non-profit organisations have identified, not least because they often develop an exceptional competence in their chosen issue in a way companies do not have the inclination or capacity to do.

The great strength of modern non-profit organisations is that they are often closely focused on a single issue and come to understand it in great depth. They often have specialists on the ground dealing with issues that neither companies nor governments fully understand, and who should therefore be heard. Companies now exist in a world where there are multiple non-profit organisations at home and abroad monitoring their every move; with modern communication systems, news travels fast and mass media outlets are only too pleased to give publicity to the stories they want to tell.

As the state has declined and non-profit organisations and companies have grown in importance, the traditional stakeholders in a company's activity have now been joined by activist organisations that want to hold companies to account on economic, social and environmental grounds. These groups are rightly claiming the space to be part of the dialogue about humanity's future, but they cannot be solely responsible for doing so. It is unfair to ask them to be leaders on the great issues of our day; they lack resources and, in many countries, are subject to active persecution in a way that companies are not.

Over the past few decades, the global rise of the non-profit sector has raised issues for authoritarian governments in particular, especially when a local non-profit organisation is linked with an international agency headquartered elsewhere. There is a natural desire for local non-profit organisations to benefit from early work done by a parent body overseas, and many international non-profit organisations are very keen to fund, develop and empower local agencies to pick up the work they have been promoting elsewhere. However, this can be seen by some national governments as interference in their national affairs and they are hostile to such international agencies. One of the things that multinational companies can do is to use their worldwide presence to help national non-profit sectors grow and link them with international equivalents as part of strengthening society around the world.

CHAPTER 4

The World
Has Changed

Introduction

History is important as it shows us where companies have come from, and the record of their contribution to society is not all bad. Furthermore, in the history of the modern economy there have been many examples of how the founders and leaders of companies have voluntarily used their power to have a positive impact on the lives of people and the natural environment. In *The Enlightened Capitalists*,[28] James O'Toole provides many examples of how business owners, founders and managers have voluntarily tried to bring social responsibility and sustainability into their businesses. He starts by reviewing the work of Robert Owen at New Lanark Mills in 1800, and goes on to look at the contributions to society of many company founders and leaders.

He cites JC Penny, Milton Hershey, John Lewis, Lord Lever of Lever Brothers, Marcus Sieff of Marks & Spencer, the Hass family of Levi Strauss, and more recently Anita Roddick and Bill Norris of CDC. He identifies one thing they all have in common, which is a belief in the ethical and human value of their business activities, and as he says of Robert Owen that even in an 18th-century factory:

> In essence, Owen thought the workplace was where the foundation of a just and reasonable social order could be laid. His commitment to human development stemmed from the same Enlightenment-era sources that had inspired Jefferson, forty years

earlier, to propose a right to the pursuit of happiness. In granting that right to his workers, Owen also anticipated the modern economic concept of 'human capital'.

When Owen was developing his sense of social responsibility to be expressed through his business, he was primarily oriented towards his employees, but he also gave thought to his customers and other stakeholders. In his day, human beings were often seen as a mere adjunct to expensive machines and much less important as a result. Owen ran a successful and profitable business, but even so tried to develop a humane working culture and vibrant community in New Lanark where his business was based. As a result, he was reviled by other industrialists as a 'socialist', and by Marx and Engels as a 'capitalist exploiter'. Nevertheless, he and the other enlightened capitalists have over time shown what a traditionally constituted private company could voluntarily do to act responsibly.

Thinking about the future, we need to recognise that over the past 70 years the world has changed in many ways. In my lifetime, the dominance of manufacturing industry in the UK, which represented 48% of the economy in 1948, has declined. It is now about 13%. Today we in the UK live in a service economy, which comprises about 80% of GDP. In the US, the figures are similar, with about 75% of GDP in the service sector. Consequently, the corporate boast that "our people are our best asset" is now true. The service sector is dominant in the economy, and in that sector the engagement of employees with the company they work for is vital for its success. For so many companies today, their people are much more important than their machines in ensuring success.

In addition, we have a much better educated workforce today than in Victorian times, and about half of 18-year-olds in the UK go to university. As potential employees, these highly educated people have choices about where they will work, and companies seeking talent need to be able to demonstrate to them that the company values social responsibility and sustainability. This is because these young people are thinking about the next 70 years, which is their future. Similarly, the surge in the growth of socially responsible consumption and investment, provides evidence of a much greater awareness in society of how companies are behaving. There is a broadly based desire in society for companies and brands to contribute to solving society's economic, social and environmental problems.

Also, humanity has begun to develop some universal standards of behaviour for governments, companies and others around the world. The publication of the United Nations' Universal Declaration of Human Rights in 1948 (General Assembly Resolution 217A) was a remarkable achievement, and it remains a benchmark for good behaviour by businesses, governments and others around the world. There are many modern international standards arising from it, such as the UN Global Compact and the Sustainable Development Goals, and these are helping define behaviour towards people and the environment in a way that did not exist 70 years ago.

These standards are more easily enforced as the world is now so intimately connected through the internet and social media. A western company with a supplier that behaves badly towards employees in China may find that those workers can get support from campaigning non-profit organisations in the west at the touch of a phone button. The type of visual images that galvanised public opinion against the slave trade in the 1790s now galvanises the public against deforestation and child labour in west African cocoa farms and south-east Asian factories. The early global economy of the British East India Company had no agreed standards of business behaviour and business communications that took six months to connect London with Calcutta. That world has now been replaced with a much more connected one.

This connectivity is also fuelling a rapid rise in the rate of change as well as facilitating global business communications. It is changing the way we live in little-understood ways. In 1990, eBay had only 82 million users but by 2010 its user base had grown tenfold. WhatsApp has gathered 400 million users in just five years and all around the world people are interconnected as never before. These sorts of changes, and many more not discussed in this book, require us to think again about the role of capitalism and private companies in a modern society; the old solution of abolishing it just will not work. Capitalism and private enterprise are back and we have to learn to live with them.

Furthermore, when *The Communist Manifesto* was published, there were about 1.3 billion people on the planet. Today there are around 7.7 billion, and the UN estimates that the world's population will increase to 11 billion by 2050. Most of these people will be poor and live in developing countries; they represent a great new market for companies, as they will want to consume many of the products and services that companies offer (TVs, fridges, cookers, mobile phones, bikes, mopeds, cars, better food and foreign travel). The pressure of the growing human population on the natural environment is already immense, as we reshape the world for our purposes, and it will only get worse with the climate crisis relentlessly developing.

In past decades, capitalism has shown that it can be far more socially inclusive than the Marxists ever thought it could be, but it seems that it cannot bear the environmental cost of its success and we must find a way to make it work for the common good as well as for private benefit. There will always be arguments about economic fairness and social justice, and the creation and distribution of wealth in society. However, where the environment is concerned, arguments about human impacts end when a species is extinct, or when the climate heats up by three degrees. There is no going back, and further argument is too late; it is pointless. Consequently, the recognition of today's environmental crisis presents a real and unavoidable challenge to humanity in general and the resurgent business world in particular.

The effects of global warming and the coronavirus pandemic are also showing us that our sense of community is necessarily becoming global. Individual countries and societies cannot just solve problems like the coronavirus and climate change for themselves and ignore the rest of the planet; governments have a key role to play in confronting these and other issues, but companies also have a key role to play. They more than governments have pioneered the growth of the modern global economy, and where the environment is concerned, the economy is the central issue.

The Emergence of Environmental Awareness

With the emergence of the global environmental crisis since the 1970s, we have seen a fundamental change in our world over the past few decades. We had always known that industry and private businesses created localised environmental damage, but it was probably with the publication of Rachel Carson's *Silent Spring*[29] in 1962 that unease about the much wider, global environmental impacts of industry began to be articulated. Her book moved the debate beyond environmental conservation, beyond a concern for saving specific local environments and species, to present a critique of the total impact of industry and modern agriculture on the natural environment generally.

At the beginning of her book, Carson says:

> The history of life on earth has been a history of interaction between living things and their surroundings. To a large extent, the physical form and habits of the earth's vegetation and its animal life have been moulded by the environment. Considering the whole span of earthly time, the opposite effect, in which life actually modifies its surroundings, has been relatively slight. Only within the moment of time represented by the present century has one species – man – acquired significant power to alter the nature of his world.

Carson's critique not only exposed the impacts of chemicals such as DDT on the natural environment but also great failings in how corporations saw their role in society. They took a narrow view of responsibility and wanted to give consumers only what they needed to address a specific problem. Companies paid little regard to the wider environmental impacts their products might have. It was left to independent scientists and non-profit organisations to identify the negative impacts of industrial innovation. Many companies would dismiss these external diseconomies on the grounds of protecting the greater good of the greater number, by securing humanity's food supply, for example.

By the late 1980s more and more large data sets were becoming available on issues such as carbon in the atmosphere and we started to see the negative impact which both communist and capitalist systems were having on the global environment. Companies in the free-market system work with very fine divisions of labour, and are tightly focused on singular objectives, such as meeting consumer needs and shareholder financial expectations. Consequently, they were blind to their wider responsibilities to the environment; often they lacked the scientific capacity to identify them, and had little idea how to form coalitions in society to address them. They were happy just to do business; if a product was legal, they went ahead and produced it for sale.

In Asia, for example, fast-moving consumer goods companies have achieved wonders in getting soap and other vital hygiene supplies to poor people by putting them in small and affordable plastic sachets. The use of plastic packaging has been central to the success of many such companies. But there is no significant refuse collection in countries such as Bangladesh and Indonesia, so the plastic packaging ends up in the rivers of south-east Asia and then the Pacific Ocean, which is being swamped by plastic waste. It is devastating ocean life forms. Today companies cannot ignore the societal failure to deal properly with the waste they create. So, in partnership with national and local governments, non-profit organisations and others in the industry, companies must step up and take a lead in helping to resolve the problem: developing biodegradable packaging for small sachets is a good idea but it needs to be adopted quickly. Similarly, companies need to be supporting the development of significant recycling initiatives as well, particularly in developing countries. Either way, the company's knowledge, skills and connection to the consumer, are a vital part of solving the problem.

Learning From the CFCs Crisis

An early example of companies being forced to face the impact of their activities on the global environment came in 1974 when two chemists at the University of California published an article in *Nature* magazine detailing the threats to the global ozone layer from chlorofluorocarbons (CFCs), and the issue was identified as important. In 1985, British scientists had found a hole in the ozone layer above Antarctica and the issue could no longer be avoided by humanity or the companies that produced CFCs.

CFCs were useful to humanity; they were legal and widely used in fire extinguishers, electronics manufacturing and items such as fridges that were vital to improving human life, particularly for poor people around the world. They were also used as propellants in deodorants, hairspray and other products not so vital to human wellbeing. It is worth considering what happened with CFCs and the ozone layer, because it may teach us something about the role of governments, non-profit organisations and companies in confronting these global environmental threats.

Most of the CFCs in the world were manufactured by publicly listed companies such as Du Pont in the US, which had about 50% of the US market and 27% of the global market. But other companies, including Allied Signal and British ICI, also made them. In the early stages of the debate about their use, Du Pont in 1980 led the formation of the Alliance for Responsible CFC Policy, and this body lobbied against drastic changes in CFC production on the grounds that the science was not conclusive and there were no viable alternatives to the existing product.

However, once the research showed conclusively that the harm to the ozone layer was directly linked to CFCs, Du Pont switched its argument and became an advocate for control. By 1986, the company had acted in its own self-interest and had filed new patents on alternatives to CFCs, as its old patents for Freon production had run out in 1979. The company became one of the parties contributing to the UN treaty-making process and seeking even tougher controls on the production of CFCs than required by the Montreal Convention on Substances that Deplete the Ozone Layer. The CFC producer companies had to become part of a tripartite effort by governments, independent scientists and others in the non-profit world to solve the problem.

The world still needed fridges, after all, and companies knew how to make them and sell them cheaply. Margaret Thatcher and Ronald Reagan were key players in the Montreal process, and despite their free-market ideas sought to address this market failure that clearly threatened the global common good. Mrs Thatcher in particular played a key role in developing the access to funding necessary to help developing economies, such as India and China, that were desperately trying to get cheap fridges to their people to improve their wellbeing, meet the costs of phasing out CFCs.

As a company, Du Pont eventually supported a global solution to eliminate CFCs and to promote the introduction of alternatives, and thereby avoided a competitive advantage going to other companies operating in other jurisdictions that still allowed the manufacture of CFCs. However, the company continued making CFCs into the mid-1990s, arguing that its customers, including the US government, wanted them. Consequently, its overall record on the issue is very mixed.

In her article, 'Ethics of Du Pont's CFC Strategy 1975–1995',[30] Brigitte Smith says of Du Pont's approach:

> Du Pont should reprioritize stakeholders, and balance the needs of human life on the planet with shareholders, rather than hold shareholders above all others. Further, it should search for solutions where the needs of both can be satisfied simultaneously. In this instance, CFCs were a very small portion of Du Pont's sales and profits, and considerable positive public relations could have been generated through an earlier and more decisive phase out of CFCs.

Smith argues that profit maximisation was behind Du Pont's attitude to the problem, but that seems unlikely given the relatively low level of revenue and profits from CFCs as part of the company's overall product range; the 'profit maximising' motive, as Smith suggests, looks too simplistic. Indeed, Du Pont says as much, and points to the needs of society to have a smooth transition to more benign products as the major reason for not immediately stopping production. But in trying to protect its relatively small amount of commercial self-interest, the company missed the point of the debate, which was about moving very quickly to protect the whole planet.

On the other hand, the electronics industry, which was a big user of CFCs, responded by coming together, led by companies like IBM, AT&T and Northern Telecom, to form The Industrial Cooperative for Ozone Layer Protection (ICOLP). It helped develop technological solutions to the problems posed by phasing out CFCs. It also made the ideas and technology transfer open source and non-proprietary, such that companies of all sizes around the world could use them quickly. The electronics industry owned its share of the problem and, in the interests of the global common good, acted quickly and decisively to phase out CFCs while giving advice to firms of all sizes and types how to proceed.

Today this is what employees, customers, consumers and the general public now expect of companies: a traditionally defensive view of commercial self-interest is not acceptable to people where it threatens the environment and human life. The outcomes of the Montreal Convention and subsequent developments have been generally positive and to some extent it is a model of how humanity can get the government, non-profit organisations and businesses to work together to address global environmental issues. As a result, CFC use has declined dramatically worldwide, and there has been a degree of repair to the ozone layer over the poles.

Nevertheless, CFCs are still produced and used, for example, in aircraft fire suppressant systems. Scientists reported that around 7,000 tonnes of CFCs had been released in eastern China in 2013, showing that enforcement of the Convention is still a problem. Enforcement now rests with governments, and such action is difficult internationally. Having said this, some positive lessons can be taken from this early experience of facing up to global environmental problems, and they may help with the even larger problems of climate change and declining biodiversity.

First, the CFC problem was global and could not be solved by the action of a single country. When a global solution is required, governments, companies and non-profit organisations all have a role to play in shaping the solution.

Second, the companies that produced the CFCs – or today, the oil, coal, gas and other sources of carbon that adversely affect the climate – have to be involved in any dialogue seeking to solve the problem. Tackling carbon emissions will be much more difficult for companies such as Shell, Exxon and Saudi Aramco because carbon production is 100% of their business, not 2% to 3% as in the case of Du Pont and CFCs. However, they understand the demand for and global uses of energy and this knowledge is vital in rapidly reducing humanity's commitment to burning fossil fuels. Even oil companies have the capacity to pioneer alternative energy sources and as energy companies they have the business interests in doing so.

Third, the global enforcement of low and zero-carbon strategies, along with other moves to protect the environment, need to be enforced effectively alongside the rapid introduction of alternative energy and changes in agriculture. The Montreal Convention on CFCs showed what can be achieved at the global level in setting standards and goals. Once a standard is agreed and set, as it was at the UN Framework Convention for Climate Change in Paris, then the three formal sectors, along with the informal sector and public at large, have clear targets to work towards and can be held accountable for their performance. Companies like targets and performance measures; it is the everyday reality of running a business.

Lastly, the dynamism and relative speed with which the three formal sectors came together to deal with the CFCs crisis could well have lessons for how humanity tackles economic and social questions too. The UN has recently published its Sustainable Development Goals after a wide-ranging consultation that included some major businesses. Is it possible that these 17 goals could provide the framework for much more collaboration between the three formal sectors in addressing a wide range of problems, including economic and social ones, which are key to the development of global society. The business community certainly needs to look to them for guidance on priorities for future action and engagement, as should governments and non-profit organisations.

Capitalism is Only a Part of the Problem

Modern capitalism often gets the blame for creating global environmental decline because it is driving and sustaining the latest wave of 'consumerism' around the world. It is indeed good at giving rich and poor consumers around the world what they need and want. It is more inventive and efficient at creating and distributing consumer goods and services than any other system humanity has tried, and this process can be self-indulgent and very wasteful. Many in the west believe that capitalism relies on relentless advertising; an issue worthy of much more discussion than is possible here, and there is a bigger question to consider about human behaviour.

As Paul Hawken says in *The Ecology of Commerce*: [31]

> If capitalism has a pervasive myth, it is the tacit assumption that business is an open, linear system: that through resource extraction and technology, growth is always possible. In other words, there are no inherent limits to further expansion, and those who wish to impose them have a political agenda.

Hawken articulates a basic concern about capitalism seen in the west and there is a great deal of truth in what he says. However, the myth he speaks of is one of human consciousness and not just a capitalist one. Capitalism is just the modern expression of that consciousness, but the world's environmental crisis has been coming for a long time. The process of degrading the natural environment began long before modern capitalism and it also went on relentlessly under communism and socialism. The private sector today happens to be central to the modern way of meeting human needs and wants, but human beings as a species have been reshaping the natural environment since they emerged on the planet.

The world's environment is a vast, self-regulating, interconnected system for life. It is human beings, with their wants and desires, that is the cause of the problem. We as a species have from our earliest days endlessly sought to arrange nature and the resources of the planet to suit ourselves, especially since the worldwide development of farming when mankind ceased to be hunter-gatherers. This development was the major intervention in humanity's relations with nature and the start of the journey towards modern societies.

Even before the emergence of farming and settled communities, humans were changing the environment around them to sustain themselves and it is human relations with other species which tell a woeful story.

In *Sapiens: A Brief History of Humankind*,[32] Yuval Noah Harari discusses the impact of human settlers on the environment, and the biodiversity of Australia some 45,000 years ago:

> The moment the first hunter-gatherer set foot on an Australian beach was the moment that Homo sapiens climbed to the top rung in the food chain on a particular landmass and thereafter became the deadliest species in the annals of planet Earth.

He argues that Homo sapiens – using only wood and stone tools, but also fire to clear the forest – was largely responsible for the extinction of 23 of the 24 Australian animal species weighing 50kg or more. Of the Americas, which were colonised some 16,000 to 14,000 years ago, he says:

> Within 2,000 years of Sapiens' arrival... North America lost thirty-four out of its forty-seven genera of large mammals. South America lost fifty out of sixty.

Coming more up to date, he says of New Zealand:

> The Maoris, New Zealand's first Sapiens colonisers, reached the islands about 800 years ago. Within a couple of centuries,

the majority of the local megafauna was extinct, along with 60 per cent of all bird species.

In the modern era, the Hudson Bay Company and other traders decimated the beaver populations of Canada and North America, basically to provide smart hats to the population of Europe. In the US, entrepreneurs initiated the mass slaughter of buffalo to provide consumers with robes, while the slaughter of whales in the 19th century was to provide lamp oil for people around the world. The discovery of mineral oil in the late 19th century did something to ease this slaughter. These impacts on biodiversity are indicative of the changes that our species has brought about over time; we have been utterly ruthless in exploiting nature.

None of these comments are designed to exonerate modern capitalism from its role in the current environmental crisis. Capitalism and the companies that make it work have come back to dominate society around the world just when the system of mass production and consumption is facing its greatest ever crisis. Paul Hawken is right; the whole model of free-market economic activity exploiting nature has in recent years hit the environmental buffers and a new approach is vital. This is at a time when around the world a vast number of new companies are being created.

If they function effectively in the future, companies will need to step up and become initiators and leaders in environmental conservation and economic and social development, rather than just waiting for governments and non-profit organisations to pressure them into action. This means having the capacity to identify the issues that matter and a proactive capacity for action either as individual organisations or in partnership with others, as the next two chapters explore.

Companies Have Been Changing Too

Not only has the political, social and environmental context in which companies operate changed over recent decades, but companies themselves have been changing and becoming much more international in origin. The Fortune Global 500 lists the biggest multinationals every year and it is a good indicator of how the world of international companies is changing.

In 2019, the top 10 largest companies listed now comprise three Chinese, three European, two American, one Japanese, and one developing country-based company (Saudi Aramco). Over the past 40 years or so, there has been a shift from US domination of the Fortune list to a European one, and now a surge of developing country companies are coming to the fore, led by the Chinese.

Despite a long history, multinationals are no longer largely the product of industrialised or western countries. While private companies of all sizes are now found pretty much everywhere around the world, they are not all set up in the same way. Each country has a somewhat different way of defining and regulating its companies, and these companies have different cultures. A Japanese company, for instance, has a different ethos from an American one. Capitalism is not a monolith; it is made up of a wider diversity of businesses, which have distinct national cultures influenced by the type of society in which they are established. The moral and other values of that society, often based on diverse religious traditions, have a profound impact on how companies see their role in society.

Charles Hampden-Turner and Fons Trompenaars were early explorers of this issue in their seminal book, published in 1993, *The Seven Cultures of Capitalism*.[33] Based on an extensive survey of managers' attitudes, it looks in depth at how national values shape the culture of business enterprises in seven developed countries including the US, Japan, the UK and Sweden. The thesis they developed can today be much more widely applied to countries such as China and India, as well as to smaller countries such as Malaysia, where religious and business scholars are writing extensively about how to blend the values of modern private enterprise with the country's traditional Muslim values.

In their book, Hampden-Turner and Trompenaars discuss the question about the origin of ethical and cultural values in a national culture and how they drive wealth creation and company culture:

> In our survey of 15,000 executives we found that culture of origin is the most important determinant of values. In any culture, a deep structure of beliefs is the invisible hand that regulates economic activity.

Despite these differences in background and culture, companies around the world work very closely together and in 2013 UNCTAD published a report that suggested that multinationals were responsible for about 80% of world trade and that about 60% of this trade, or $20tn, was intercompany trade within the value chains of multinationals and others.[34] This ability to cooperate between companies of different nationalities and cultures is a remarkable example of global cooperation between peoples with different cultures. Today companies don't fight one another with armies and navies; they do compete, but they have also developed an extraordinary capacity for international collaboration and this capacity has the potential to work very much to humanity's advantage.

While not commenting directly on capitalism and international trade, Yuval Noah Harari makes an observation that is highly relevant to how companies behave in society, in *Sapiens: A Brief History of Humankind*:[35]

> Money is the only trust system created by humans that can bridge almost any cultural gap, and does not discriminate on the basis of religion, gender, race, age or sexual orientation. Thanks to money, even people who don't know each other and don't trust each other can nevertheless cooperate effectively.

In the past 40 years, and despite significant cultural differences, companies have adapted to the multicultural demands of the modern global economy. Many western multinational companies have been spreading knowledge and skills and setting standards of behaviour around the world; this is potentially important in developing corporate responsibility and environmental sustainability worldwide. Many developing world companies, for example, want to be accepted as being 'world class', so they invest heavily in becoming as commercially competitive as developed world companies, but have also addressed issues such as child labour and deforestation, because that is what world-class companies are now expected to do.

Many western multinational companies have adapted to the global market by creating codes of conduct and statements of ethical values, which managers around the world are expected to adhere to. These codes often include economic, social and environmental issues, and in this way multinational companies are encouraging the spread of progressive business values around the world through their management, and the education and training of their employees.

This is important because companies have become the world's great system builders. They create integrated systems that can move a piece of sweetcorn grown by a small-scale famer in Kenya, who may well be Muslim, to the shelf of a London supermarket, and on to the dinner plate of a middle-class, Christian consumer, in 36 hours. Companies move goods from China and India to shops all around the world and from workshops in Dhaka to fashion stores in New York in days. The multinationals have become the great global connectors of societies; they have been quietly getting on with developing international agreements and understandings with one another, and integrated systems with a multitude of small supplier businesses around the world.

We need to learn how to exploit these capacities for the global common good, not least because the other two formal sectors don't know how to do this sort of thing. The international non-profit organisations and NGOs take up a large amount of airtime in the public discourse about humanity's future, but when we examine their international activities, they are largely a collection of individual projects that are unconnected with one another. The projects may be worthwhile in themselves, but they are not part of a system of change. Similarly, governments may be party to international treaties and agreements, but their capacity to act on issues is so often limited to their own national jurisdiction. Multinational companies and their international connections bring something different to the table.

An Empowered Population

There is one global trend in addition to those mentioned above that is of real importance as we think about the role of companies in society in the future. Not only do we have a better educated population than in the past, but also the recent empowerment of ordinary people through access to unprecedented forms of mass communication; this is linked to the steady decline in deference to authority that is seen in the west and around the world.

Modern social media have empowered ordinary people in an unprecedented way, and mass communication has really come to the fore in society. They have become key to setting a global agenda for responsible behaviour by governments, companies and non-profit organisations. Vast numbers of those in poverty now have mobile phones and the Arab spring was organised through mobile phones, as were the demonstrations in Hong Kong and many of the Black Lives Matter movement. These developments allow ordinary people to challenge authority in governments and companies too. In addition, around the world there is a growing disdain for the type of 'benevolent paternalism' that was once a key feature of political and corporate life. This change has implications for how companies think about and act on their responsibilities in the world; this is discussed further in **Chapter 6.**

An earlier generation of business leaders – including Robert Owen, Lord Lever, the Cadburys, Carnegie, Ford and Hershey – sought to do well by their workers, but they did so in a 'top-down' spirit of benevolence. They acted towards them as fellow human beings worthy of consideration in their own right and voluntarily used their power in the business in line with their personal values to reflect a social responsibility agenda, and we rightly respect them for that. However, the future will require companies to have a much broader base of engagement by its various stakeholders when they address corporate responsibility issues.

Allied to this decline in the acceptability of benevolent paternalism, there is also a growing spirit of 'equality of value' for people around the world, between the most wealthy and powerful of the US, for example, and the poorest of human beings living in Africa and Asia. Across companies there is a growing recognition that top-down organisations need to have a flatter structure, and that all employees need to be involved in organisational success. Companies are not just about the pursuit of profits; they are communities of people working for a common end.

Companies also exercise power in society, and increasingly the corporate social responsibility and sustainability movement needs to recognise that this power must be more broadly shared in the company and across society. In a global company, corporate leaders cannot know what goes on in the business at a local level all around the world; and they cannot know the nuances of local culture or the details of local business activities. Consequently, they need to devolve responsibility for corporate responsibility and environmental sustainability decisions, just as they do other business decisions.

Corporate leaders today can set the commercial goals and articulate the ethical values of a company, but they cannot manage all the detailed decisions required to run the business. Its employees and other stakeholders can. This is one reason why codifying company values or articulating its purpose clearly is crucial in getting local managers and employees to live out these goals and values. When a business is small and local, entrepreneurs and managers can exert a direct influence on how it behaves, but once it becomes a large, international company, then systems must be in place to make sure it lives its values and meets it responsibilities to stakeholders and the wider society.

Given how the world has changed in recent years, particularly with the growing environmental crisis, it has become vital to look at ways of engaging our companies, and the empowered people who work in them, in the common struggle to address the issues ahead of us. We need to mobilise our growing community of businesses around the world to join in constructive partnerships with governments, the non-profit community and the people seeking to address our economic, social and environmental challenges. The next two chapters look for a way forward. Companies are just too powerful and creative not to be fully engaged in consciously shaping the world's future.

CHAPTER 5

A New Social Contract with Business

Introduction

The time has come when humanity must honestly accept that we want capitalism and private companies to be part of the mix of institutions operating in our various societies. We want what companies can give us and, in return for the freedom, they must be creative and innovative, but this is just one side of the bargain. Companies must correspondingly accept an obligation to act with careful and constant regard to society's urgent economic, social and environmental problems.

We are not going to get rid of companies as the Marxists tried to do, but we must fundamentally rewrite the social contract between companies and society worldwide. This contract must apply to each and every company, and oblige them to help humanity face its economic, social and environmental problems.

Corporate responsibility and sustainability have, in the past, been developed on a voluntary basis by charismatic individuals who have used their business to express their own deeply held values. From the days of

Robert Owen, through to the Cadburys and Lord Lever in Britain, Robert Bosch in Germany, the Tata family in India, through to modern-day entrepreneurs, such as Anita and Gordon Roddick of the Body Shop, and Ben and Jerry of ice cream fame, it has so often been the conviction of the owner or founder that has driven the corporate responsibility agenda. These individuals and their companies have chosen voluntarily to act responsibly, and they did so because of ethical conviction, not because the law required it of them.

What they have done is to show us what companies can achieve as a force for good when they set out to do so. My former employer, Levi Strauss & Co, ran a garment business. As the company expanded after the second world war, it built new factories in the Deep South of the US, bringing much-needed modern industrial employment to deprived communities. However, racial discrimination was endemic, and the leaders of the company saw what was happening and set out to integrate its plants in the 1950s. This was done with little disruption, and in doing so the company showed what could be achieved in terms of the equality of employment for African Americans; once Levi Strauss had integrated its plants, no one could say it could not be done.

In *The Enlightened Capitalists*,[36] James O'Toole rightly praises the efforts of such people as the Levi Strauss management team:

> I admire the moral courage these men and women have displayed when doing what they felt was right, whatever the personal cost. Some of them have been, I admit, a bit quirky and obsessive, and a few utterly eccentric; nonetheless, to the extent that I have heroes, they are mine. They represent the promise of a virtuous corporate capitalism that the idealistic side of me finds socially and economically desirable.

He goes on to say, however, that when these leaders retire, die or sell their business, the values they have so often championed decline and disappear. We can no longer rely on a small number of enlightened corporate leaders who voluntarily commit their companies to responsible and sustainable behaviour. We must make such a commitment an integral part of the constitution of every business.

So how do we redefine the social contract between business and society in terms of a legal and moral obligation to humanity? Humanity has invited companies back into the centre of global society to do what they do well, and it is worth reiterating that the price for the freedom they have been given must henceforth be matched by an undertaking on their part to address the economic, social and, especially, the environmental consequences of their activities. They must be legally bound to address the challenges of our time, in partnership, when necessary, with the other two formal sectors.

We can no longer talk about capitalism and the functioning of a market economy just at an abstract level, as economists and others are prone to do. We need to see that the companies that make capitalism work are key units of social organisation, that they are communities in themselves and that they can be mobilised to help confront society's problems and secure the planet's future.

Just over 27 million people work in the for-profit sector in the UK, which represents about 80% of the total working population. More than 7,500 large companies (defined as more than 250 employees) employ 10.7 million workers and generate nearly a half of the sector's turnover. If these companies alone were to be required to focus seriously on managing their social, economic and environmental impacts, that change would bring profound benefits to society and the environment. Furthermore, it is not just the large companies that can make such a contribution; the ideas set out in the rest of the chapter are equally applicable in principle to small and medium-sized businesses.

Companies and the Public Interest

We must start thinking of companies as communities of people who, in their own way, can also work for the public good as well as meeting the wants and needs of the marketplace. That means embracing the work they do in the marketplace, while at the same time requiring them to be proactive in addressing the economic, social and environmental issues that they and society face. This in turn means that as part of the contract between society and the company, each company must have an explicit commitment to economic, social and environmental responsibility and to promoting the public good beyond its work in the marketplace.

Today the state is still seen as the final arbiter of public good and will involve itself in regulating companies on key issues. For example, it forbids child labour and the adulteration of food products, and sets minimum levels of workers' pay. However, the state must now change the law to require companies to be proactive in helping society to face its problems. As companies differ in size, function and global reach, there is a limit to the level of detail that can be specified in any law and the state will always have a role in regulating the behaviour of companies on specific issues. However, companies should know that, in principle, they need to make appropriate arrangements for acting in a social and environmentally responsible way according to their circumstances.

In _Company Law_,[37] Alan Dignam and John Lowry note that charter companies were created by a 'concession' from the state to pursue a specific business purpose, but go on to discuss the impact of the change to companies that had a purely private status in the 1850s:

> ... as incorporation became available to all rather than just those deemed worthy by the state. The state provided the general framework for incorporation but was no longer involved in the detail of each corporate venture. Significantly it gave up the ability to set the objectives of a corporation. This was now done by those setting up the company and framed in terms of their own private needs in the objects clause.

Around the world, the state has accepted that companies are a key part of developing human civilisation and is willing to let them have considerable freedom to show creativity and to serve the population through the marketplace. However, in return for the freedom to do so, companies must in future be required to use their immensely creative abilities to address society's wider problems as well as operating through the commercial marketplace. This means that all companies must now accept that in addition to their commercial purpose, which is a matter entirely for them, they must also by law have a corporate responsibility and sustainability strategy to complement what they do as commercial entities.

We are not going to take away the independence of companies, but add a specific responsibility as part of incorporation, to pay proper regard to the economic, social and environmental impacts of the business and its role in wider society. At this point in human history, the time has come to place a legal obligation on all companies to be good corporate citizens.

Because companies differ in character, size, scope and purpose, each one should be charged with the general responsibility to define what this means for them. Companies should then be given the freedom to develop the policies and practices that give expression to their distinctive corporate responsibility and sustainability profile. Companies should also be obliged to report annually to society on what issues they have identified as being material and what they are doing to address them. They should show, with good data, how effective their efforts have been.

Time to Change the Law

Companies are already subject to a great deal of legal control, nationally and internationally. Examples include a labour law which says that a company must provide a safe and healthy workplace for employees and pay the national minimum wage. There is a great deal of corporate law on how the business must be run; there is tort, contract and tax law, environmental laws and even criminal law, which covers issues such as fraud and corruption. However, what is proposed here is to change the very status of the company as a social institution, not merely specific aspects of its behaviour.

In the UK, the Companies Act 2006,[38] which came into force in 2009, sets out the governance of private companies. It sets out what a company is and how it should be governed, as well as the rights and duties of shareholders, directors and even creditors. It also specifies how publicly listed companies may raise money and the levels of transparency to which different types of companies must adhere. It is over 700 pages long and describes in great detail every imaginable aspect of creating and running a company, from the definition of purpose, naming, keeping the records, reporting company activities and the role of directors and shareholders.

In the UK's Companies Act 2006, the company is seen as a private enterprise and its purposes and goals are to be determined by its founders and owners. But Article 172 of the Act explicitly requires directors of companies to take account of stakeholder interests and the economic, social and environmental responsibilities of a company; and these concerns are set in the context of the success of the business, not the success of society and the wellbeing of the environment. Actual reporting on how the company meets the requirements of Section 172 is not expected until 2020 so it is hard to say exactly what impact it will have on businesses, but it is doubtful that it will be substantial.

In the Act, it is assumed that companies will pursue a commercial purpose within the law, and with all the flexibility that the law allows. While Section 172 of the Act is a nod in the direction of corporate social and environmental responsibility, it is not a strong statement of a new social contract between business and society.

This situation must change. What is required is the reformulation of our whole idea of the role of a company in society and the law must make a substantial change to the legal requirements made of companies as social institutions. We must see companies simultaneously as private enterprises responding to the marketplace and as social institutions committed to pursuing the public good.

New legislation of substance must be introduced to require all companies, certainly the large and medium-sized ones, and perhaps to a lesser degree the small ones, to have an active policy for managing their economic, social and environmental impacts in society. The deal with companies for the future is simple: society wants you to remain free to do what you do well in the marketplace, but in return society will impose a general obligation on companies to engage consciously with the wider impacts of their business activities, do something about them and report annually on their activities.

What is suggested here is not that companies are forbidden to do something, but that they are asked to go on the front foot and make their own plans to help achieve the positive changes that society needs. Humanity now needs companies not only to use their creativity in the marketplace but also to use it in seeking solutions for social and environmental issues. They cannot do everything, but they have the scope to do a great deal about issues with which they are especially connected.

What matters is that we seek to change how companies see their role in society as commercial and as social institutions. We need to embrace the remarkable contribution that companies make to our civilisation and then move them a step further toward engaging constructively in the processes of social change and environmental protection. This is a step change to the status of companies, and an amendment to the Companies Act 2006 need not be lengthy; a short new section will do the job, but it needs to articulate fully a new vison of the role of business in society. It won't solve all humanity's problems but it will make a useful contribution.

There is a whole book to be written on the detail of such a change. What precisely companies will be asked to do and how is not for discussion here. However, it is time to acknowledge that along with the state and non-profit sectors, companies can serve society through their work in the marketplace and their commitment to social responsibility and sustainability. There will be problems of enforcement, and there will be companies who will do little or nothing, and many in the business world will be strongly opposed to such an idea, but the price of economic freedom for companies in the future must be social responsibility and sustainability. With respect to environmental impacts, the need for this responsibility is desperately urgent.

As the regulators of companies, governments are tentatively beginning to move in the direction of having companies do more for society, but it tends to be on an issue-by-issue basis. Politicians have big social and environmental agendas and they increasingly have come to recognise that they cannot achieve them without the newly expanded private sector. Consequently, they are starting to put wider responsibilities on companies to be good citizens.

In the UK, we have the example of Section 172 of the Companies Act 2006. In India, the government has amended its Companies Act 2013[39] to require companies with a net profit in excess of $700,000 to establish a social responsibility committee and contribute 2% of their profits to what is called corporate social responsibility activities. The emphasis is on the philanthropic activities of companies rather than the broad-based view of corporate responsibility in which philanthropy is just a small but valuable part.

The UK government also introduced the Public Services (Social Value) Act 2012,[40] which requires public authorities and crown services to "have regard to the economic, social and environmental wellbeing in connection with public service contracts". This means that large city councils spending money on goods and services can weight contract decisions in favour of companies and others offering 'social value' as part of their commercial bid.

Many companies that do a good deal of business with governments – such as Sodexo, which handles outsourced services, Balfour Beatty in construction, and Legal & General offering financial services – have already responded to this requirement in order to be able to do business with government agencies. However, pressures like these from governments are not fundamental shifts in how they see the role of companies in society, as they are not promoting a fundamental change in the constitution of companies to include an obligation to address a broad range of economic, social and environmental issues.

Companies have lived through great changes in business culture before and have survived. Companies are some of the world's great problem-solvers and a legal requirement to address a company's economic, social and environmental impacts will hopefully bring forth some major innovations. Corporate social and environmental responsibility is not new; it just needs to become the normal way of doing business for all companies, not just a few leaders in the field.

Companies Will Resist Change

Many companies will tend to resist the imposition on them of a new set of legal responsibilities, and their views need to be considered. They will tend to take a very traditional view of their role as serving the society in which they operate through the marketplace, and they won't want to be distracted from it. At least two major concerns about such a change need to be addressed: **first,** a tendency to instinctively reject extra regulation; **second,** fear that additional responsibilities will necessarily damage the business and require additional expenditure.

Regarding extra regulation, there will indeed be substantial new obligations placed on companies. Companies will not lose any of their existing freedoms to do business, but they will, in addition, have to work out what corporate responsibility and environmental sustainability means for them and develop policies to respond to their analysis. They won't be burdened with detailed regulations, but will be given additional responsibilities that sit alongside their normal business activities.

In addition, many companies, large and small, have already picked up the challenge of trying to manage their business in a socially responsible and increasingly sustainable way, so not a lot will change for them. Many companies are already working through, on a voluntary basis, what the 'circular economy' and 'conscious capitalism' mean, as well as responding to ISO 9000, BS 8900, the Global Reporting Initiative (GRI) and other standards for responsible behaviour. By legislating for a change to affect all companies, we would in fact be creating a level playing field across businesses in respect of companies paying regard to social and environmental responsibility.

For example, many of our largest companies now voluntarily produce social responsibility and sustainability reports to increase transparency about their sense of economic, social and environmental responsibility. GRI reports that more than 250 of the world's largest companies voluntarily report their economic, social and environmental performance using its standards. This means that these companies are already thinking about the issues, working on them and trying to measure performance against standards agreed in the multi-stakeholder format of the GRI. Extending this sort of reporting to all companies may well seem burdensome to many, even if they don't use the extensive measures set out by GRI; such reporting is the price they will have to pay for their licence to do business in future.

Walmart is the world's largest business (by revenue), and it has its finger on the pulse in terms of what consumers are thinking. It has taken steps to require that all its suppliers meet certain social and environmental standards before the company will do business with them. Walmart is not the only retailer to take such steps and this is because retailers, above all other businesses, are close to the public and they sense the changing mood in society and know that companies must adapt to it. Pressure is building on businesses for economic, social and environmental responsibility from within the business community itself, not just from governments.

The investor community, for example, has also picked up on this modern trend and has responded by creating a field of 'socially responsible investing' (SRI) to cater for investors to ensure that their money is not being invested in companies harming people and the planet. It is estimated that over $20tn of investments are now made with regard to the environmental, social and governance (ESG) performance of a company. In recent years, many listed companies have developed the capacity to report against ESG measures, and companies have been steadily developing the skills necessary to meet an obligation to creatively manage economic, social and environmental responsibility over recent years.

Generally speaking, leading companies like level playing fields in business. This is why they often support legislation on issues: it is the laggards that don't, and there are plenty of them. However, the laggards have some excellent role models and plenty of knowledge and experience to draw on as they are pushed to step up and join the movement towards a better future. The voluntary movement to embrace a modern version of corporate responsibility and sustainability has its own momentum because more and more businesses recognise that consumers don't want products that have been produced in an exploitative way or that damage the environment. Similarly, bright young people don't want to work for companies that do economic, social and environmental harm.

The wind of change that has restored companies to a prominent role in so many societies has also brought with it a desire by ordinary citizens to have those companies behave in a modern way. By writing that commitment into law, and despite creating additional burdens for some companies, society is creating a place for companies that will take them safely into the future.

The second reason for company resistance to change is the concern about additional costs imposed on them by the new legal obligations. There may well be such costs on some on occasions, but it is a mistake to think that commitment to corporate social and environmental responsibility always increases costs: it doesn't. There are several ways of looking at the problem of costs in the economic, social and environmental fields and we deal with them next.

1. Companies Can Save Money

A great deal of environmental innovation has saved companies money by reducing the demand for water, electricity and the use of landfill, for example. There may well have been some initial expenses to put environmental programmes in place, but the (often capital) costs of these initiatives amortised over time has saved the company money.

On the social side, I saw that by providing basic healthcare and simple family planning for young women in garment factories, absence from work was significantly reduced, productivity improved and the company gained from the additional performance. When we ran the numbers, it was clear that the costs of the programme were easily covered by increased profitability.

Similarly, when companies provided health education and condoms for male workers during the HIV and AIDS epidemic, they deferred the costs to their healthcare insurance of having to care for a large number of infected individuals. It should be remembered that in some developing countries over 20% of the population were infected and the impact on a mine or factory workforce could be devastating for productivity. This was in addition to the healthcare costs that most companies incurred, since around the world, businesses pay healthcare costs for employees. There was a strong incentive to control costs, unlike in countries where free healthcare is provided to employees by the state.

2. Social and Environmental Responsibility Can Help Build a Business

Early Quaker companies (such as Cadbury, Rowntree's and Clarks shoes) were founded on their owners' integrity in terms of price, quality and the treatment of their workers, and prospered as a result. More recently, Ben & Jerry's (the ice cream business), Anita and Gordon Roddick's Body Shop and Innocent Drinks are examples of businesses founded on strong principles of social and environmental responsibility. As part of their business offer to consumers and employees, they have incorporated significant aspects of economic, social and environmental responsibility into their core business practices, and these companies have done well as a result.

Corporate responsibility is not the only way to build a business, as the Haagen-Dazs ice cream producer demonstrated. As a major competitor of Ben & Jerry's, it sold its products using some very sexy advertising, a good old standby for getting consumer attention. However, it is possible that integrating social and environmental responsibility into the core activity of the business can be just as successful in promoting growth, particularly in this modern world where consumers and workers are looking for corporate responsibility as an integral part of a brand's and company's culture.

Interestingly, all three firms mentioned above were subsequently bought by multinational companies – Unilever, L'Oréal and Coca-Cola – which, as global businesses, wanted to showcase in their portfolio the type of approach these smaller companies represented. Today, companies such as Patagonia, which is close to its consumers, are taking significant steps, through their websites and other means, to let consumers know just how responsibly and sustainably their products are produced. Corporate responsibility can be key to brand identity and certainly helps maintain a connection with socially and environmentally aware consumers.

This trend of publicly demonstrating corporate responsibility is found in many consumer-facing companies. They are starting to emphasise, through advertising and public relations, the social and environmental credentials of their products. Professor David Grayson and Adrian Hodges have discussed this in *Corporate Social Opportunity! Seven Steps to Make Corporate Social Responsibility Work for Your Business*[41], which reviews how economic, social and environmental responsibility can be a business opportunity for a company. As ever, though, there will be exceptions. While the idea of building the reputation of a company and its commercial success through corporate responsibility can have a wide application, it is not necessarily appropriate for all companies.

3. No Costs Are Involved

Some things a company can do to address economic, social and environmental problems have no costs. For example, when Levi Strauss integrated its plants in the Deep South of the US no significant costs were involved; the company's leaders just had to have the will to confront one of the most difficult social problems in the US. The company may have indirectly benefited from workforce integration by creating a larger labour pool from which to draw its workers, but the company's leaders acted because it was the right thing to do and cost was not a consideration. It was a values-driven decision.

On the other hand, there were some commercial risks involved in the potential reaction of plant communities, and perhaps even the marketplace, because at that time most of Levi's customers were young American men aged from 15 to 25, and in the 1950s many of them would perhaps have disapproved of the company's action. Similarly, when Bob Haas, the chief executive in the late 1980s, took a stand on HIV and AIDS in San Francisco, when the issue was very controversial around the US and the world, he did so as a commitment to basic human rights. The minimal costs involved were not a consideration.

4. Modest Costs and Big Impacts

My first experience of seeing extra costs being incurred by Levi Strauss to address an urgent social issue was when the Northern Europe Division closed its North Shields plant in 1983. The total closure budget was in excess of £2m for redundancy costs and other expenses, but the president of the division, Robin Dow, authorised me as community affairs manager to spend an additional £50,000 to help with the community impact of the closure.

The closure was going to add to the local burden of unemployment, but with a small increase in budget over and above the legally required costs of the closure, we were able to work with the local authority and Project North East, a local charity, to ease the problem of unemployment and help our own workers. We put in place a series of local job creation initiatives, including setting up a workers' sewing co-operative and a computer skills training project to help some of our workers and other community members make the transition to higher-skilled jobs. This was a positive response to the changes in the marketplace and the capitalist system generally, which obliged Levi Strauss to get out of manufacturing.

In California, Chevron wanted to create greater access to work in the oil industry for women and did so by using charitable funds to support primary and secondary school courses aimed at promoting science for girls. The company then created a university-level scholarships scheme with the same aim. It cost money to do this sort of work, but the costs were relatively small and the social benefit substantial. In my home town of Nottingham, it was a local businessman, Jesse Boot of Boots the Chemist, who substantially met the costs of building the local university. Many such examples of corporate philanthropy can be found around the world. While his company received some indirect benefit from the university's creation, such as a pool of qualified employees and having a community more attractive to managers, the costs incurred led to a huge community benefit.

5. Some Costs are Real and Substantial

It would be wrong to suggest that the costs of doing the right thing in respect of economic, social and environmental issues will always be small, cost-free or have offsetting economic benefits to the company. Sometimes they don't, and a company may well have to absorb significant costs to do the right thing. If a company has to recall a product or stop manufacturing a profitable one (such as CFCs) because of environmental concerns, it will face some losses of income and profits. While working for Golden Agri-Resources in Indonesia, I saw the company set aside some of its valuable land holdings for conservation purposes in response to Greenpeace and other protesters seeking to retain the rainforest. Other companies have stopped doing business in South Africa under apartheid and Myanmar under the dictatorship and have lost business as a result.

In addition to incurring direct costs, there may well be opportunity costs that a company could forego. For example, there may be a loophole in tax liability and transfer pricing policy which the company could quietly and legally take advantage of, but should it? Similarly, what does a company do about increasing pay to shrink the gender pay gap? Will the company pay the 'living wage', or just the national minimum wage as required by law? There can be real costs involved in these business decisions.

There is one important further cost, which many large companies are already embracing: the cost of complying with new obligations. Changing the contract between business and society will impose some modest costs of compliance on all businesses. There could well be a cost for defining, managing, monitoring and measuring the process of corporate responsibility and sustainability, particularly for larger multinational companies. These management costs will not be large and may well be absorbed into the existing management structures of smaller companies, but multinationals in particular may well need some specialist staff to help with identifying and responding to economic, social and environmental challenges.

Managing Corporate Social and Environmental Responsibility

In addition to the costs of organising their commercial mission, companies will in future need to know how to fulfil this new, obligatory role of social responsibility effectively. They will need to develop a whole new management discipline concerned with economic, social and environmental responsibility. This new step in the evolution of company identity will require them to include managing corporate social and environmental responsibility alongside the commercial objectives of the company. This can be compared with companies that have over the past decades built the human resources function as a professional discipline; indeed, it has been less than 100 years since the whole discipline of modern management science was created.

While a business is small and is based in one country, the company's leadership team can have a good feel for a range of issues to be considered beyond the commercial goals of the business, but once a company becomes large and global, the leadership team needs specialist support in addressing a whole range of issues. A corporate leadership team based in London, San Francisco or Delhi cannot know what issues a company needs to address in dozens of different countries. While line managers can help a lot, because they are often very close to social and environmental problems the company needs to address in their country, a wider range of professional research and knowledge is often needed. Just as a company pays for advice from lawyers, accountants, marketing people and human resources consultants about running the business, in future large companies will also need to make provision to get the best advice on the economic, social and environmental issues facing it.

Even in the 1980s, Levi Strauss had already established a senior management committee called the Corporate Responsibility and Ethics Committee to provide specialist advice to senior managers as they made key business decisions. The committee was made up of the senior officers of the company and included a non-executive director; my job, with others, was to help the committee make ethical decisions on big issues such as disinvestment from South Africa, the community impact of plant closures and how to respond to the HIV and AIDS epidemic.

As enlightened capitalists, Peter and Walter Haas, the leaders of Levi Strauss, knew that they needed a certain amount of research, advice and support to make good decisions about economic, social and environmental issues. They knew how to run a clothing business, but knew about as much as the average citizen of the US when it came to a wider range of economic, social and environmental issues around the world. So they took steps to institutionalise the availability of such advice to the business.

In the 1980s, Levi Strauss had a worldwide workforce of over 20,000 people; those of us who worked for the Social Responsibility and Ethics Committee never numbered more than four or five. Nevertheless, we were a cost to the business, but we helped, through research and other means, to provide due diligence, on an important aspect of the company's impact on the world.

Just as the finance department gave advice to the company about finance, the lawyers about legality, the market researchers about growth market development and the human resource department about people policies, the corporate responsibility function gave advice about the social responsibility and environmental aspects of business decisions. We were just another corporate function, sometimes in conflict with other corporate functions over decisions to be made, but at other times helpful in supplying solutions to problems that these other functions faced.

In the future, all large and many medium-sized companies will almost certainly need to have a special capacity to manage their economic, social and environmental profile with the same degree of care that they apply to commercial challenges. We urgently need to create within the corporate community a distinct discipline trained in managing corporate social and environmental responsibility. Just as with other corporate functions, there is a distinct body of knowledge to be mastered and skills developed.

Companies have managers and employees at many levels around the world who already know a lot about the issues in their society, and their expertise can be vital. As is the case with company leaders, their view of the issues is often constrained by their experience and tight focus on commercial goals. A central corporate responsibility function needs to be there to offer support to them too, acting as internal consultants to the business. Line managers around the world who are struggling with ethical, social and environmental responsibility issues need to be able to turn to the central function for support in thinking them through.

Within a company, the social responsibility and sustainability unit also has a horizon-scanning function, identifying key issues and probably establishing a dialogue with the non-profit organisations concerned with them. Such organisations are often at the leading edge of thinking about problems and proposing responses. Their single-issue focus is often a great strength in this context as they develop great in-depth knowledge and skills on the chosen issue. Just as companies maintain links with politicians and regulators, they also need to develop links with forward-thinking social organisations of all sorts dealing with emerging issues that may well have cost implications for the company.

If in future companies are to report on their corporate responsibility and sustainability, as well as their financial performance, then drawing this material together in a coherent way is another task for a corporate responsibility function. It really helps develop a dialogue with society. Should companies embrace this role, they will be serving the public good in their own way, just as the government and the non-profit sector do in theirs. That should diminish the suspicion of their role in society and give them a place in its development that puts them alongside the other two formal sectors, and will show that they do not solely serve their narrow self-interest and that of their owners.

The Importance of Values

We can change the social contract between companies and society such that their licence to operate includes a legal requirement to pay regard to the ethical, economic, social and environmental issues. We cannot – and should not try to – legislate for each individual company's distinct set of responsibilities. An oil company has a different business profile and set of issues from that of a hotel business, for example. We can put into law only a general injunction requiring responsible and sustainable policies and practices; the range of different companies is just too diverse for detailed legislation. Once companies know they have to account for their performance in these matters, they will have to work out for themselves what they must do, and how they will do it.

Absolutely key to that is that a company will need to be clear about the values it will live by while pursuing its particular commercial mission. Having a clear set of values is fundamental to working out what a company stands for and what it must do about the issues it encounters in its business life. Some argue that this is about defining the 'purpose' of the company, but it is clearer to think about a company having a commercial mission allied to a clear set of ethical values that guide its business decision-making while pursuing it.

For example, a company may want to be the world's best and largest maker of jeans, but its values should say, "Not at any price." It will respect human rights and not source from suppliers that use child labour, and it will minimise environmental damage such that it will not use cotton grown in an environmentally destructive way. All company founders and leaders have values, and those values have in the past permeated a company's culture. Whether they are made explicit or not, everyone in life has values. They are integral to life for individuals and institutions.

In future it will be essential for companies to reflect on their values and make them explicit so that all who work for the company or do business with it know what it stands for. This is a challenge for companies and businesses of all sizes, even small ones, such as independent shops and sole traders. They all need to be clear about where they stand in terms of society's ethical, economic, social and environmental concerns and then be able to justify their values and communicate them.

In many respects, values are what tie a company together, and they are the foundation of action when shaping the company's relationship with society. For example, Vodafone as a global company has a mission to be one of the largest and best providers of mobile communications services on the planet. It is now a huge, global business and every effort is directed towards making this commercial vision a reality. However, it also espouses certain key values, which are embodied in its code of conduct,[42] and these ethical principles are there to guide the company's decision-making alongside its commercial business decision-making. It wants to be the best in its industry, but not at any price. It has set out a statement of ethical standards and says why it has a code of conduct:

> Our Code of Conduct sets out what we expect from every single person working for and with Vodafone. It underlines our responsibilities to our people, partners and shareholders. Our Code of Conduct helps us all to make informed decisions and tells us where to go for more information.

The code goes on to give guidance on issues such as bribery, money laundering, abiding by competition policy, diversity in the workplace and managing environmental impacts. As a large, international company predominantly built by acquiring overseas businesses, Vodafone espouses values that help to bring a consistency and uniformity to its corporate identity around the world. They show newly acquired companies that Vodafone is not just an economic force: it knows it is a social one too, and needs to manage that aspect of its impact on the world as well as its commercial impact. From a business point of view, it needs trust from all its stakeholders and the wider society to operate effectively, and that is in large part created by its behaviour as a good corporate citizen set out in the code of conduct.

A good model of a simple and clear statement of values is the one that guides the international pharmaceutical company, Johnson & Johnson (J&J). The company has a long history of making products for babies and infants, so parents need absolute trust in the efficacy and benign nature of those products. The emergence of the credo[43] as a values statement for J&J is instructive; it was first drafted by the founder's son, General Robert Wood Johnson, in 1943, as the company started to grow internationally and just before it went public. It was not called a credo until 1948, but it made explicit the values that had guided the company as the owning family built the business. Robert Wood Johnson was in effect telling potential investors, other stakeholders and the wider world what the company stood for and what it in turn owed to each of its stakeholders.

As the company has grown around the world, this credo has been translated into more than 36 languages and dialects so that it is accessible to all employees and others in society. **Box 1** below quotes the credo in full, and it is interesting to see that it pledges to give stockholders a "sound profit" and a "fair return", not a maximum one.

We believe our first responsibility is to the doctors, nurses and patients, to mothers and fathers and all others who use our products and services. In meeting their needs everything we do must be of high quality. We must constantly strive to reduce costs in order to maintain reasonable prices. Customers' orders must be serviced promptly and accurately. Our suppliers and distributors must have an opportunity to make a fair profit.

We are responsible to our employees, the men and women who work with us throughout the world. Everyone must be considered as an individual. We must respect their dignity and recognise their merit. They must have a sense of security in their jobs. Compensation must be fair and adequate, working conditions clean, orderly and safe. We must be mindful of ways to help our employees fulfil their family responsibilities. Employees must feel free to make suggestions and complaints. There must be equal opportunity for employment development and advancement for those qualified. We must provide competent management and their actions must be just and ethical.

We are responsible to the communities in which we live and work and to the world community as well. We must be good citizens – support good works and charities and bear our fair share of taxes. We must encourage civic improvements and better health and education. We must maintain in good order the property we are privileged to use, protecting the environment and natural resources.

Our final responsibility is to our stockholders. Business must make a sound profit. We must experiment with new ideas. Research must

---

be carried on, innovation programs developed and mistakes paid for. New equipment must be purchased, new facilities provided and new products launched. Reserves must be created to provide for adverse times. When we operate according to these principles, the stockholders should realize a fair return.

Credo is a Latin word that means a set of beliefs, and it is widely used in a Christian religious context. In J&J's case, they are beliefs on which people base their lives, ones that help guide their actions. In effect it says to employees that when they are in doubt about issues in business and society, they should look to the credo for guidance. Corporate policies can change relatively quickly, but corporate values tend to develop more slowly over a longer period, as they did with J&J's values statement. For example, in 1979 as environmental issues became more prominent, the company added a reference to protecting environmental resources. Then, as American society changed and women went out to work more often, the company added the word 'fathers' alongside 'mothers' in its first sentence about commitment to consumers and others.

The credo was adapted to changing social values because companies not only help shape society, they also need to respond to the evolution of social and environmental ideas. Although the J&J credo was initially written for a family-owned pharmaceutical company, as it changed and grew, its core tenets could be adopted by many companies, large and small. It represents a clear articulation of the values and beliefs that guide the business as it pursues its commercial mission.

Chart 5 below sets out in a diagram, the **Values Cascade** where, in the role of a values statement, it is integrated into the management strategy of a company such that ethical, economic, social and environmental issues are seen as a normal part of business activity.

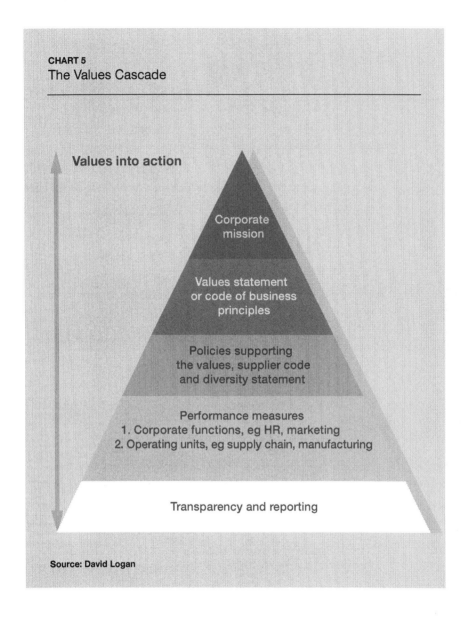

CHART 5
The Values Cascade

Values into action

Corporate
mission

Values statement
or code of business
principles

Policies supporting
the values, supplier code
and diversity statement

Performance measures
1. Corporate functions, eg HR, marketing
2. Operating units, eg supply chain, manufacturing

Transparency and reporting

Source: David Logan

As **Chart 5** suggests, a company must go beyond having a values statement like J&J's (which of its very nature must be rather broad and aspirational) and develop practical policies to ensure that its values are lived out in reality. The point of having an explicit commitment to a set of values is that the company can seek to manage them over time, just as it does with commercial challenges. Ethics and values do not exist in a purely abstract form: they must be made concrete and practical to be real. Consequently; this allows them to be measured and their success in living them out evaluated.

It is fine to say that the company is committed to the principle of a safe and healthy workplace, but there need to be policies in place to ensure that this principle is achieved on the ground. The impact of these policies needs to be carefully measured to show that they are effective, and if they are not then something needs to be done to make the necessary improvements. With health and safety at work, data about fatalities, lost time, accident rates and ill-health retirements, for example, all indicate whether or not the values are being lived out. The figures for each measure can be benchmarked against external norms to show whether the policies are effective or not. There is a lot of science, detailed knowledge and skill involved in gathering the data at every stage and developing and deploying resulting policies.

Generally speaking, different parts of the business, such as human resources, finance and supply chain management functions, will each be responsible for drawing up the policies derived from the company's values and making sure that they are implemented. However, it will tend to be the corporate responsibility and sustainability specialists who are responsible for collecting this information across stakeholder groups and communicating it to the wider world in a comprehensive way, often through a corporate responsibility and sustainability report.

Such transparency and public reporting is essential if the company is to develop trust with its stakeholders and the wider community. Companies cannot always be right and perfect in their performance, but they need to be open about the issues and dilemmas they face. If society wants companies to be better and more active citizens, it is going to have to come to terms with the many dilemmas that companies face while running an international business. To do that, the other two formal sectors and the public at large all need to be better informed about the day-to-day realities of business life. Corporate responsibility and sustainability reports help to do that.

Whether we like it or not, private companies will be central to shaping humanity's future, and this chapter has set out some of the key changes necessary to prepare them for that wider role in society. If they are to have the freedom to go on doing what they do well in terms of providing goods and services in the marketplace, society has a right to require them to take on a new obligation to manage their economic, social and environmental impacts with greater care. In this way, humanity is acknowledging the value companies bring to society while asking them to be partners in humanity's economic, social and environmental development.

Companies must now be brought into the debate about humanity's future. The next chapter looks at how they might play that role in our emerging global society and what these changes mean for modern capitalism.

CHAPTER 6

Facing the Future

Introduction

With continued population growth, the consumption of goods and services is going to go on growing substantially around the world. It is not just a problem of advertising driving excessive consumption in industrialised countries, as many claim. There are issues here, but also huge latent demand for greater consumption in developing countries, and companies will continue to serve society through providing goods and services in the marketplace. The economic 'hidden hand' of Adam Smith's private profit-seeking activity by companies will continue to contribute to society.

The previous chapter argued that companies should be able to retain their ability to create and advertise new products and services and, in this way, meet human needs, wants and aspirations if they also take on board the need to do so in a socially and environmentally responsible way. Companies are designed to create and exploit market opportunities, but the whole of society needs to discuss and act on the wider questions raised by the free-market, capitalist system. Since humanity around the world has opted to invite capitalism and companies back into our societies, we should at least try to engage with the companies in paying regard to the public good as part of their normal commercial activities.

If the role of companies can be more broadly developed, then the future of the planet is set to be one of more partnerships between the three formal sectors being applied to the resolution of humanity's challenges. **Chapter 3** pointed out that as governments retreated from a dominant role in controlling the economy, the for-profit sector and the non-profit sector emerged as powerful forces in shaping humanity's future. It is these three sectors, allied to changes in how people in the informal sector live, that will drive change.

The three formal sectors, as shown in **Chart 2,** (page 60) each interact with the people in the informal sector in different ways. Each of the formal sectors has a distinct contribution to make in shaping humanity's future. **Chart 2** also shows the three formal sectors overlapping and by implication working together, and this is a vital part of the puzzle for the future. We have learned that no one sector has the whole answer to humanity's issues, but the combined experience of the three is much more likely to help society find solutions. A great challenge is to get these three sectors to understand one another better and to start working together effectively – locally, nationally and internationally.

Although companies have been part of human society since the beginning of recorded history, they have generally not seen their role as being one of proactively promoting the public good, beyond activity in the marketplace. Where they have gone further and addressed wider social and environmental issues, it has tended to be at the instigation of enlightened corporate leaders who have acted voluntarily according to their values. However, now is the time to require all companies to take up a wider role in promoting the public good as the price for having the power and freedom to operate commercially. There are many things that companies can do themselves, but they must also learn to join the other two formal sectors in partnership where necessary.

If companies are legally required to step up and accept a responsibility to manage their affairs with regard to economic, social and sustainability issues, two things can happen:

> **First,** the enormous power and innovative capacities of the private sector will become increasingly engaged in trying to resolve many of humanity's problems.

> **Second,** as companies become overtly committed to economic, social and environmental responsibility, they may well be better able to form partnerships with the other formal sectors to promote action.

Three Perspectives are Better Than One

Companies will need to become clear about what they can do by themselves in the course of their normal commercial activities, what they can do in partnership with others, such as government and non-profit organisations, and what others must do. Companies cannot do it all and they need to set limits on their commitments and be prepared to argue for them, but central to their contribution will be what they can do through their business activities to promote economic opportunity, social development, human wellbeing and environmental sustainability. The second area that holds rich opportunities for the future is in developing partnerships with the other two formal sectors, as the overlapping circles in **Chart 2** show.

Each of the formal sectors has distinct bodies of knowledge and skills that, when constructively brought together to address issues, can produce much more powerful outcomes than if just one sector alone were left to address a problem. Three perspectives will always be better than one. Because of their specialist knowledge and experience, non-profit organisations and governments often have perspectives on problems that companies don't have, as the example of the CFCs crisis showed. Input from governments and non-profit organisations can have a real value to companies in managing issues, because companies tend to be very tightly focused on their core commercial activities, and as a result miss important issues as they emerge. One of the strengths of our civilisation is its fine division of labour, but that is also one of its great weaknesses.

However, building alliances across sectors is not easy. Each of the three formal sectors has a distinct culture and language, and attracts different types of people to work in them. Getting them to work together can be difficult, but it is precisely those differences in experience across the three formal sectors that can contribute to the problem-solving process. What is critical for companies is that they now need to bring their businesses fully into society's problem-solving process. The other two organised sectors will have their issues with companies, and vice versa, but these differences cannot be allowed to block the dialogue process.

Currently this is not always the case, because many people in the government and non-profit sectors still see companies as purely an expression of a private desire for profit at any price, rather than organisations that can serve the public good. On the other side of the coin, many corporate executives tend to see the other two formal sectors as being staffed with barely competent do-gooders who don't live in the real world. Clearly, they must work together as problem-solving forces and cannot continue to think and act as distinct and separate systems.

As companies come to this world of global dialogue, they bring two distinct capacities:

> **First,** there is the behaviour of the company itself as a corporate entity, a citizen of society, and this is most important because it has a huge and direct impact on society and the environment.

> **Second,** there is the role of the company in enabling its stakeholders and others in society to be good citizens themselves. Precisely because we do have a much more educated and globally connected population, companies increasingly need to see their role in terms of engaging stakeholders and those they interact with in the process of directly addressing social and environmental issues. The next section of this chapter looks at how companies can fulfil these two roles and become much more of an active citizen of our global society.

Companies as Good Citizens

As the agents of the market system, companies are organised entities that have 'agency', that is, the power to do things for good or ill. At the core of this power are the commercial activities of the company in providing goods and services to the marketplace. They have choices about how to behave while pursuing these commercial goals, and a clear statement of values will help guide those choices. When they apply their values, not only in the owned and operated business of the company, but also right along the whole value chain, from raw materials to production to consumption and to product disposal, they can have a massive impact on society.

Today the idea of corporate responsibility and sustainability has expanded beyond issues within a company's owned and operated business to include how the company's commitment to values plays out along its value chain. Companies are increasingly seeking to ensure that raw materials suppliers, manufacturers, wholesalers, retailers and the consumer are involved in their corporate responsibility and sustainability strategy; this is a positive development.

To take an example from one industry, **Chart 6** below provides a map showing how the scope of corporate responsibility and sustainability looks today for a modern food company. It identifies representative examples of economic, social and environmental issues in the backward linkages to suppliers as well as in the forward linkages to consumers. This sort of map can be replicated for every type of business, not just one providing food, but as an industry it is a good example of how thinking about corporate responsibility has developed in recent years. It allows a company to begin to see its place in society in relation to the total footprint of the business, whatever types of goods and services it is offering in the marketplace.

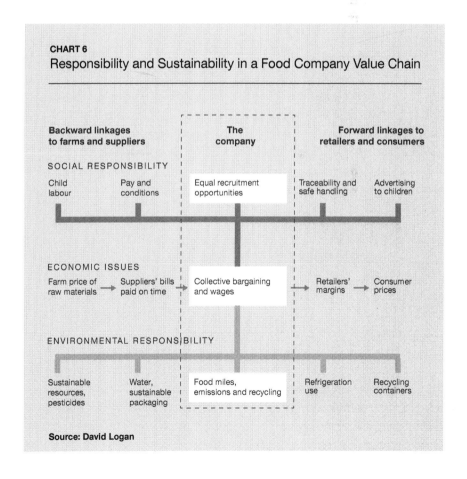

CHART 6
Responsibility and Sustainability in a Food Company Value Chain

Backward linkages to farms and suppliers		The company	Forward linkages to retailers and consumers	
SOCIAL RESPONSIBILITY				
Child labour	Pay and conditions	Equal recruitment opportunities	Traceability and safe handling	Advertising to children
ECONOMIC ISSUES				
Farm price of raw materials	Suppliers' bills paid on time	Collective bargaining and wages	Retailers' margins	Consumer prices
ENVIRONMENTAL RESPONSIBILITY				
Sustainable resources, pesticides	Water, sustainable packaging	Food miles, emissions and recycling	Refrigeration use	Recycling containers

Source: David Logan

In the social strand of **Chart 6,** child labour, for instance, is identified as an issue in the production of agricultural raw materials such as cocoa. Non-profit organisations working in west Africa campaigned on the issue because they had far more people observing conditions on the ground in the cocoa-producing regions than the companies sourcing raw materials from there. The non-profit organisations, rather than the companies, were the experts on social and environmental conditions in the cocoa-growing regions. They saw the problems, such as child labour, and through the media created sufficient concern about it in US and European markets that the confectionary and other food companies had to respond rapidly and actively. Similarly, in industrialised country markets, at the consumer end of the value chain, other non-profit organisations have highlighted the impact of sugary drinks, confectionery and processed foods on childhood obesity and diabetes and subsequently forced changes in company advertising to children.

The economic strand of **Chart 6** identifies the prices that poor farmers get at the farm gate, and the issue has led to the emergence of the non-profit Fairtrade movement as a counterbalance to the normal operations of free-market economics. At the other consumer end of the value chain is the issue of food prices for consumers, which has been explosive in developing countries where food riots are not unknown due to high prices for staples such as palm oil, grain and rice. Golden Agri-Resources, a company producing palm oil, has worked closely with religious and other organisations in Indonesia to ensure a cheap and reliable supply of palm oil to local consumers.

The environmental strand of **Chart 6** identifies the use of pesticides as an issue because governments in the US, Europe and Japan have been pressured by activist non-profit organisations to ban the organochlorine pesticide Lindane from use. Public health testing showed that some residues of the pesticide were to be found in cocoa sourced from west Africa, a real problem for multinational companies trying to source raw materials from millions of small farmers there. African farmers producing cocoa have used Lindane in the past and, despite a ban in Ghana, for example, some still use it today. It is cheap and effective from the farmer's point of view, but because of international standards (Japan rejected a shipment of cocoa beans in 2006), companies have had to engage in helping resolve the problem locally.

In respect of the environmental concerns for consumers in **Chart 6,** the issue of recycling plastic and other containers used to sell foods and soft drinks is really pressing all around the world as this branded plastic rubbish is washed down rivers to the oceans. Many companies, including Coca-Cola, have seen the need to respond and have done much to promote the recycling of aluminium cans. Companies are aware that they have created this waste and cannot just leave it to governments to remedy. Furthermore, the non-profit organisations that rightly campaign on the issue don't have the capacity to work at scale to solve the problem, but companies do. Leading companies are already developing biodegradable packaging for some products as well as supporting recycling schemes; governments may well step in to make these measures compulsory.

Some companies will respond to these problems by changing suppliers, ceasing to produce certain products or changing their formulation and changing their packaging. These can be positive moves but don't solve the general problem in society. Such measures can clean up a company's or brand's value chain and consequently enhance their reputation, but in the future companies will need to solve the problem for themselves as businesses and will also be expected to use their knowledge and skills to help society to solve the problem generally. They will often do so by developing long-term partnerships with the government, non-profit organisations and others that have the knowledge and skills to help them address the issue.

Working in Partnership

This section takes the food industry example, extrapolates the ideas further and looks at how all sorts of companies can work in partnership to effect change. These ideas are relevant to all industries. Furthermore, it is important to note that companies need to work with one another to solve problems. Some elements of competitive advantage can be derived from being a leader in social and environmental responsibility, but many of the problems that companies face are not specific to a particular company or brand: they are industry-wide problems. Consequently, it makes sense for the companies to work together to help solve them.

For instance, the alcoholic drink companies have long been criticised for the social impact of alcohol and, while individual companies have their own programmes, the industry came together some years ago to form the International Centre for Alcohol Policies (now called The International Alliance for Responsible Drinking). Through the alliance, these highly competitive companies developed common approaches to issues such as drink-driving and underage drinking. The formal private sector drinks industry across North America, Europe and Asia has come together to offer its response to society's problems. Despite criticism of industry involvement in these sorts of issues from public health activists in particular, it is a positive development that needs to be built on; not least because these companies know a great deal about consumer behaviour, and that knowledge needs integrating into public health thinking.

When a leading company such as Unilever has identified an issue of importance to business and society, the company has often taken the initiative and done something about it in partnership with other companies and stakeholders. As well as securing the commercial interests of Unilever as a business, these initiatives try to solve the problem for society generally. The foods side of the business – like the home and personal care side, which has a similar record – has over the years consistently found creative partnership responses to social and environmental issues in the raw materials supply chain of the company's brands.

In 1966, Unilever responded to UN and international concern about dwindling fish stocks and joined the World Wildlife Fund (WWF) to launch the Marine Stewardship Council (MSC) to address the worldwide impact of the fishing industry. This initiative helped the company secure its goal of sourcing all its fish from sustainable sources by 2005, but also created a potential solution to a problem that was to affect many other businesses and consumers. The company helped develop the MSC as a fully independent non-profit organisation by 1999, with the goal of safeguarding seafood supplies for future generations, partly through the certification of fish sources and the labelling of products for consumers.

The MSC was consciously created as a 'multi-stakeholder' organisation from day one, a partnership that brought together businesses, non-profit organisations, governments and independent scientists to work on the problem. It reached out to fishing companies and retailers, following through to the marketplace, and sought to educate and inform consumers' purchasing preferences in the informal sector marketplace. The MSC has its problems, but it is a model of how companies can play a part in proactively helping to address global environmental issues.

In 2004, Unilever's foods business again responded to public concern and non-profit pressure, led by Greenpeace, about the impacts of the palm oil industry on Asian forests and communities. Unilever recognised that as one of the largest buyers of palm oil in the world, it had a share in the problems the crop was creating. Consequently, it helped launch the multi-stakeholder non-profit Roundtable on Sustainable Palm Oil (RSPO) initiative. It did so to help secure its own supply of sustainable sources of palm oil while at the same time changing the performance of the whole industry. The company was not just content to buy itself and its brands out of the problem, but was also seeking to make a wider contribution by addressing the problems facing the whole palm oil industry.

The RSPO has gone on, like the MSC, to become a fully independent non-profit organisation in its own right, with the participation of a wide range of global companies, non-profit organisations and independent experts and, despite some hostility from the Indonesian government (which tried to set up its own national version of an RSPO), the initiative has gone on to certify 4.22m hectares of plantations, involve 75 growers, certify 413 mills and provide Unilever and another 3,081 companies with sustainable supply certification. It is a step towards developing a sustainable supply chain for the industry as a whole by drawing on the special knowledge, skills and contacts of all three organised sectors, including governments.

A good example of how companies can reach out and help consumers is provided by the collaboration between the Grameen organisation and the French company, Danone. The Grameen Bank is a classic example of a developing country non-profit initiative. It started in 1974 to do micro-lending to extremely poor people in Bangladesh because neither the government nor the private sector were meeting their financial needs. This bottom-up approach, started by Mohammed Yunus, was a great success and the bank has over 2,500 branches. The Grameen movement later diversified into other activities, such as housing, food and village phone services.

The founder of Grameen Bank knew the grass roots problems of the poor people of Bangladesh very well and he wanted to get cheap, nutritious food to their children. So, in 2006 (the year he won the Nobel Prize for Peace) he teamed up with the French company Danone to manufacture vitamin-fortified yogurt for the children of Bangladesh. The company knew about making yogurt and Mohammed Yunus knew how to access poor consumers, and between them they founded a social business (profits are retained and used for social purposes) to manufacture and sell yogurt. The business also developed a valuable job-creating value chain, made up of local dairy farmers as raw material suppliers and salespeople employed to take the product to consumers in the villages and the slums of the cities.

The initiative has had problems with growth and distribution systems, but still represents a positive partnership between a business and a non-profit organisation where they bring together their distinctively special skills to the table to solve a significant social problem. As this and many examples show, leading companies can bring important knowledge, skills and special contacts to social and environmental problems, not only in the food industry but in virtually all industries and services. In future we need to see much more of that happening as a matter of course in communities of all types around the world.

It is not just large businesses that can make such contributions; small and medium-sized companies can too. That is true right across all types of industries, not just food companies. Back in the 1990s, I was asked to visit five BP service stations in Northern Ireland to learn about what they did, if anything, to help the community. It was remarkable what stories these businesses owners and managers could tell once asked. They did not keep records of what they did; they just intuitively used their business skills and knowledge to reach out and help address community problems. They acted without a theoretical framework of social responsibility because they felt part of the community. They could see problems where they could help, and wanted to do so.

All these service stations gave to local charities, often in the form of cash and products from their shops for raffles. They also had much more sustained commitments to helping with community concerns. One business freely offered training to young local people in car maintenance, while another organised transport for its customers to take sick and elderly local people to Belfast city hospitals. These activities were in addition to the normal commercial activities of the service stations in providing the community with oil, petrol and other services as part of business life, but they also recognised that they had a special contribution that only they could make, to certain community problems.

These activities came about because the service station franchisees and managers had a strong sense of their business being part of the local community. They therefore had the feeling that they should help the community face problems such as youth unemployment or a lack of transport for poor and elderly people. They did not see their business as separate from community life and running a service station necessarily put the business at the heart of community life. That is also true in Africa, Asia and all around the world. Indeed, truck stops in these parts of the world have been important locations for focusing anti-AIDS education among truck drivers, a key group in the spread of HIV.

This sort of engagement and partnership-building by leading companies is already happening on a voluntary basis right across a wide range of industries, and as a result they are laying the foundations for a future where it is the normal way of doing business.

Empowering Stakeholders to Be Good Citizens

Companies as organisations can act to address major social and environmental problems and they can also use their power to help company stakeholders be good citizens in their own right. It has been noted that businesses have relationships with a range of stakeholders, such as employees, consumers and communities, and precisely because companies are organised entities with special skills and knowledge, they can share their resources and what they know, to help their stakeholders. The company can be effective in reaching out to help its stakeholders and others face the specific problems and other issues in society that concern them. These may not be the issues that concern the company as an organisation, but that is not the point; it does not matter because the company strengthens society by helping its stakeholders get engaged.

Companies may help employees for business reasons by providing a range of benefits that support them, such as childcare and on-site preventative health screening, but they can go further. Companies can promote car sharing to reduce travel costs for employees and environmental pollution from cars. They can create credit unions to help with finances, organise language training for new migrants, and help provide a whole range of scholarships for the personal education of individual employees. With leading companies, time off for public service is common, as is time off for volunteering, which with matched giving programmes can support employees to do more with the charities of their choice.

These initiatives can greatly extend the ability of an individual employee to contribute to society as a good citizen and that is important when about 80% of people who work in the UK do so in private companies. The workplace remains a central social unit in our society and it is through education and action in the workplace that a great deal of social and environmental progress can be fostered.

Many such businesses have strong links with the marketplace and leading companies can support good causes that consumers are concerned about through cause-related marketing and local donations. Some supermarkets, for example, allow consumers to direct company giving to local causes according to how much they spend in store. In its early days, the Body Shop offered to refill plastic bottles so that they were not added to plastic waste. Companies such as Apple offer incentives to consumers to return old equipment for recycling by giving them a reduction on the price of purchasing new products. Banks, shops, pubs and restaurants are active in encouraging consumers to support causes such as homelessness. They are often giving out important educational information about such issues and they can play a significant role in promoting public education and mobilising public action.

Multinationals in developing countries do a lot of work in helping suppliers develop their capacity to trade with them and others. Many big companies have a vested interest in having stable and effective local supply chains overseas, with the result that some are helping small businesses grow and develop as suppliers. This makes sense for the company, and it also strengthens small businesses and the local economy through skills transfers and employment opportunities. For a small business in a developing country, winning a contract with a major multinational is a great help in developing local business contacts and the confidence of bankers and others. It greatly helps their credibility as a business, meeting international standards in the commercial world and increasingly the social and environmental one too.

In a variation of this theme, many businesses in the US run 'minority supplier programmes' to help people from minority backgrounds, including new immigrants, and female entrepreneurs become suppliers to the company. The rationale is simple: it is fine to have employment programmes that promote equal opportunity, but it is also important to help people from disadvantaged backgrounds to start and run their own businesses, and large companies offer these emerging businesses a market for their goods and services. Consequently, they need to take measures to help these small and emerging businesses to be prepared to meet company standards as suppliers. These programmes show the use of the company's place in society as an economic entity to enable wider participation in the economy by disadvantaged people.

With regard to local communities, businesses large and small have a physical presence in a huge number of them. In addition to providing jobs, supporting local supply chains and paying local taxes, these workplaces are key social centres in themselves, where employees spend about eight hours a day forming important relationships. Consequently, companies can be a powerful positive force in local communities, helping them deal with many sorts of economic, social and environmental issues.

As early as the 1980s, every Levi Strauss & Co sewing plant, distribution centre and office all around the world had a company-supported community involvement team. These were made up of ordinary workers – plant managers were specifically not allowed to sit on them – and the teams were given time off in the workplace to plan their activities. They mostly arranged fundraising activities and the company supported them by giving £4 to match every £1 they raised from sponsored bike rides, social evenings and the like. As a consequence, the small towns where the plants were often located benefited greatly from the giving of these community involvement teams. Ordinary, working-class women were empowered to be prominent philanthropists in the localities where very few other sources of funds, such as foundations, existed.

There are many such examples of companies stepping up to help their local community where their facilities are based. They act as 'local citizens' and contribute to community life through cash giving and through employees volunteering and sharing their equipment, knowledge and skills in partnership with local agencies from the public and non-profit sectors. The workplaces which companies create and maintain can be important centres of social and environmental action when the company has a policy to promote such engagement and supports it with modest resources.

Companies are not, however, expert on local issues such as homelessness, drug addiction or domestic violence, but in partnership with others who are experts, they can make a real contribution to addressing them. They can help with key issues such as providing jobs, training, and mentors for those in need; and providing good regular employment is so often key to solving local social problems. Companies can do so much to help local community stakeholders, but to do so they need to be engaged with the community and that is not always the case today. In future we want to see every business understand its place and role in the local community such that it can plan to use its resources and specialist knowledge to help them face problems and foster prosperity.

Does Corporate Responsibility Change Capitalism?

If all companies are to be more socially responsible and environmentally sustainable, whether the nature of capitalism will change is a very good question to ask. The answer at one level is, "Yes", and at another level, "No". The market economy will continue growing, changing and supporting ever-growing consumption but private companies remain the agents of the free-market system.

In the UK, there are 7,500 large companies (more than 250 employees) and 3,500 medium-sized (50 to 249 employees). These companies control a large part of our economy and employ over 14 million people. Having them change their policies and practices would no doubt have a huge impact on society. There is no doubt that if they were all to develop a policy for rapidly reducing their carbon footprint to zero, for example, they would have a major impact on the environment.

However, such a development will not in itself solve the problem of global climate change; it will only make a useful contribution to doing so. At another level, action by others, notably governments nationally and internationally, will be needed. They will need to shape the markets in which the companies are working, for example, by banning the sale of petrol and diesel cars by 2040 as the British government has done. Individual car companies may make decisions about obtaining carbon neutrality on their own, but the whole system requires overall regulation in the public interest, and that is beyond the power of individual companies.

What an expanded requirement for corporate responsibility will do is to engage companies in identifying and addressing the types of issues identified for the food industry in **Chart 6**. In that single industry, addressing the sorts of issues identified would greatly help to improve people's lives and their experience of capitalism at the grass roots level. Food companies, for example, would be required to concern themselves with issues such as fair pay and human rights in their long supply chains, and help small farmer suppliers in developing countries learn about environmental issues and act on them. A company's connection to the developing world can be a critical route for transferring knowledge and resources to poor countries. Their consumers would then know that their companies and their brands were committed to working with others in making a positive contribution to sustainable, healthy food all around the world.

Leading companies have shown how to contribute to issues as diverse as fair prices for farm crops, protecting fish stocks, conserving forests, curtailing child labour, developing cheap and nutritious products for poor children and promoting recycling. All companies must now join that effort. If they lack the expertise to do everything that is needed, leading companies and business organisations, and the non-profit community in particular, have that experience and would be there to help through positive engagement. Actions like these will change capitalism in respect of the everyday life of many ordinary people and in addition make a positive contribution to global problems. Consequently, it is possible to change and improve capitalism at the level of the individual company.

However, in the UK there are big, overarching issues associated with our food supply, and they remain in the domain of government to address. This has been the case in Britain since the 1840s when the Corn Laws were repealed, allowing cheap wheat to be imported from North America and elsewhere to reduce the cost of bread for the industrial working classes. This development was subsequently followed by the import of cheap meat from New Zealand, Argentina and elsewhere, with the introduction of cold storage on ships, a classic capitalist innovation. These two forces changed the food industry in the UK and their effect is felt even to the present day.

The changes in the Corn Laws benefited the poor consumer but led to a depression of farm prices and job losses in the British farming industry. They also caused increased dependence on foreign-sourced food, which in two world wars led to chronic food insecurity. To cope with this, the government of the day developed rationing and virtually nationalised farming and food distribution. Food security again emerged with the Covid-19 virus when panic-buying surged in UK supermarkets and private companies scrambled to solve the problem.

Rational, modern business innovations, such as 'just-in-time' logistics in the supply chain and the globalisation of supply, have made our burgeoning cities very sensitive to supply interruptions. These sorts of business decisions create serious public policy issues that will be resolved only at the national and international level by governments. Consequently, we can expect the debate about the future of capitalism to continue at this level.

The workings of the free-market system necessarily raise issues that go beyond the behaviour of individual companies. Just as individual citizens make choices that are collectively problematic, so too do individual companies as they follow market opportunities. Their collective behaviour can raise problems that can be addressed only through public policy changes. For example, individual companies may choose the use of tax havens for offshore profits, and while they can decline advice from accountants to use them, the answer to the role of tax havens in the global economy is a general one, not to be solved solely by the actions of individual businesses. There are significant limits to what the actions of individual companies can achieve as they are part of a wider capitalist system and it will remain problematic in many respects.

Learning to Live with Our Problems

In the past 40 or so years we have brought back capitalism and private business because it is good at giving us what we want and desire and, like it or not, the companies that make the system work are important expressions of human creativity, as social institutions and in the activities they undertake. They have been changing our world ever since they first emerged at the beginning of recorded history when, alongside governments, they first organised large-scale work and national and international trade.

Some will argue that significant changes initiated by individual companies cannot happen, because as profit-seeking enterprises companies will necessarily fight to go on engaging in socially harmful and environmentally damaging activities as long as they can profitably do so. They will argue that the capitalist system is necessarily flawed and must be replaced. But capitalism will go on for the foreseeable future and we need to learn to live with it. One change has been offered here that represents a step forward in humanity's capacity to live with capitalism. It does not solve all humanity's problems but at least offers a way to improve our response to them by bringing companies firmly into a coalition with governments and non-profit organisations to help face the future.

A key issue is that democratic governments, like companies, are constrained by what we the people want, and it has to be remembered that on a global basis some of the world's largest oil, airline, tobacco, and drinks companies, for example, are owned by governments. They could do the right thing and shut them down tomorrow, as many would advocate for these 'harmful entities'. But they won't, because like their private company counterparts these government-owned companies have a role to play in satisfying consumers' immediate needs and wants. Even if those immediate needs and wants are not, as in the case of tobacco, in the people's long-term self-interest.

Humanity is caught in repeating patterns of behaviour that can be simultaneously immediately satisfying and desirable but potentially very harmful in the longer term. To blame capitalism and its private companies alone for a wide range of economic, social and environmental problems, including the culture of 'consumerism', is a mistake. Individuals and families in the informal sector are benefiting greatly from the market based system that is capitalism. No product or service is offered in the marketplace unless it is to be consumed, and we the consumers, not the investors, first and foremost drive the capitalist system.

Over time the innovations that companies have brought about in society through goods, services and ancillary capacities have delivered things of immense value to humanity. They have been able to do this because they represent a distinct and devolved element of power in society, and we like it that way. While some think the answer to humanity's problems is to invent whole new economies or societies just as the communists did, this book argues that we should accept the reality of our situation and learn to work better with the private companies and other institutions we are allowing to evolve organically.

Consequently, while problems will remain with the overall system of society and its capitalistic element, the component parts of modern society, the three organised sectors, must spend time working on how to collectively address the economic, social and environmental responsibilities humanity must shoulder in order to progress; indeed, to survive. Private companies especially now need to do the work necessary to join the other two formal sectors in defining and pursuing the public good.

There are many examples of how this has been done by leading companies on a voluntary basis. We now need to legislate to change the culture around the role of companies in society, as part of the acceptability of them as a force for positive change. The society we are creating around the world will come to rest on the contributions of the three formal sectors, and by having them work in conjunction with the informal sector where individuals and families live, humanity has the best chance to help manage the conflicts that are bound to arise as part of how we organise life.

Over the past 50 years or so, humanity has made its choice about the fundamental shape of social organisation, and it is one that includes private companies and non-profit organisations. It has chosen various forms of free-market capitalism. We now need to get on with acquiring the skills and knowledge to make the organically evolving structure work more effectively. It is a practical 'bottom-up' evolutionary approach, not a 'top-down' theoretical one.

Whatever social and economic system we have, humanity around the world will always have problems, and they must be faced. But with the combined efforts of the three formal sectors we have created, companies included, we can, and will, have a much better chance of facing the future.

Notes and References

Chapter 1

1   Marx, Karl and Engels, Friedrich (1848) *The Communist Manifesto*. Reprint, London: Penguin Books, 1967.

2   Ibid.

3   Labour (1918) *The Constitution of the Labour Party*. London: the Co-operative Printing Society. (The updated version of the original clause IV is now available in the *Labour Party Rule Book 2020*).

4   Tooze, Adam (2006) *The Wages of Destruction: The Making and Breaking of the Nazi Economy*. London: Allen Lane.

5   Nicholson, Virginia (2002) *Among the Bohemians: Experiments in Living 1900– 1939*. London: Viking.

6   The Times (2020, 8 October) Attenborough: Curb capitalism to save earth.

7   https://www.edelman.com/trust/2019-trust-barometer

Chapter 2

8   Moore, Karl and Lewis, David (1998) The First Multinationals: Assyria circa 2000 B.C., *MIR: Management International Review, 38*(2), 95–107.

9   Moore, Karl and Lewis, David (2000) *Foundations of Corporate Empire: Is History Repeating Itself?* Harlow: Financial Times Prentice Hall.

10   Kriwaczek Paul (2012) *Babylon: Mesopotamia and the Birth of Civilization*. London: Atlantic Books.

11   Milton, Giles (1999) *Nathaniel's Nutmeg: How One Man's Courage Changed the Course of History*. London: Hodder and Stoughton.

12   Trentmann, Frank (2016) *Empire of Things: How We Became a World of Consumers, From the Fifteenth Century to the Twenty-first*. London: Allen Lane.

13   Rivoli, Pietra (2005) *The Travels of a T-shirt in the Global Economy: an Economist Examines the Markets, Power and Politics of World Trade*. Hoboken, NJ: John Wiley & Sons.

14   Beckert, Sven (2014) *Empire of Cotton: A New History of Global Capitalism*. London: Allen Lane.

15   Trentmann, Frank (2016) *Empire of Things: How We Became a World of Consumers, From the Fifteenth Century to the Twenty-First*. London: Allen Lane.

16 Schumpeter, Joseph (1942) *Capitalism, Socialism and Democracy.* New York: Harper & Brothers.

17 Greenspan, Alan and Wooldridge, Adrian (2018) *Capitalism in America: A History.* London: Allen Lane.

18 Harari, Yuval Noah (2011) *Sapiens: A Brief History of Humankind.* New York: Harper.

19 Dignam, Alan and Lowry, John (2006) *Company Law.* Oxford: Oxford University Press.

Chapter 3

20 De La Cruz, Adriana, Medina, Alejandra and Tang, Yun (2019) Owners of the World's Listed Companies, *OECD Capital Market Series.* Paris. www.oecd.org/corporate/Owners-of-the-Worlds-Listed-Companies.htm

21 Abrahams, Jeffery (1995) *The Mission Statement Book: 301 Corporate Mission Statements from America's Top Companies.* Berkeley, CA: Ten Speed Press.

22 Clay, Jason (2005) *Exploring the Links Between International Business and Poverty Reduction: A Case Study of Unilever in Indonesia.* Oxfam GB, Novib Oxfam Netherlands, and Unilever.

23 Seery, Emma and Caistor Arendar, Ana (2014) *Even It Up: Time to End Extreme Inequality.* Oxford: Oxfam International.

24 Stiglitz, Joseph E (2012) *The Price of Inequality: How Today's Divided Society Endangers Our Future.* London: Allen Lane.

25 The Times (2020, 23 January) Davos: Make us pay higher taxes – we can afford it, demand billionaires.

Chapter 4

26 Hochschild, Adam (2006) *Bury the Chains: The British Struggle to Abolish Slavery.* London: Pan.

27 Salamon, Lester and Anheier, Helmut (1997) *Defining the Nonprofit Sector: A Cross-National Analysis.* Manchester: Manchester University Press.

28 O'Toole, James (2019) *The Enlightened Capitalists: Cautionary Tales of Business Pioneers Who Tried to Do Well By Doing Good.* New York: HarperCollins.

29 Carson, Rachel (1962) *Silent Spring.* Boston, MA: Houghton Mifflin.

30 Smith, Brigitte (1998) Ethics of Du Pont's CFC Strategy 1975–1995, *Journal of Business Ethics, 17*(5), 557–568.

31 Hawken, Paul (1993) *The Ecology of Commerce: A Declaration of Sustainability.* New York: HarperCollins.

32 Harari, *Sapiens.* Ibid.

33 Hampden-Turner, Charles and Trompenaars, Alfons (1993) *The Seven Cultures of Capitalism.*

34 UNCTAD (2008) *World Investment Report 2013: Global Value Chains: Investment and Trade for Development.* New York and Geneva: United Nations.

35 Harari, *Sapiens.* Ibid.

Chapter 5

36 O'Toole, *The Enlightened Capitalists.* Ibid.

37 Dignam and Lowry, *Company Law.* Ibid.

38 Legislation.gov.uk, *Companies Act 2006,* www.legislation.gov.uk/ukpga/2006/46/contents

39 Ministry of Corporate Affairs, India, *Companies Act 2013,* www.mca.gov.in/Ministry/pdf/CompaniesAct2013.pdf

40 Legislation.gov.uk, *Public Services (Social Value) Act 2012,* www.legislation.gov.uk/ukpga/2012/3

41 Grayson, David and Hodges, Adrian (2004), *Corporate Social Opportunity! Seven Steps to Make Corporate Social Responsibility Work for Your Business*

42 Vodafone (2019) *Our Code of Conduct: Doing What's Right.* Berkshire: Vodafone Group.

43 Johnson & Johnson, *Our Credo.* www.jnj.com/credo/

About the Author

David Logan is a co-founder of Corporate Citizenship, an international consultancy working on corporate responsibility and sustainability. He has 40 years of practical experience in frontline corporate responsibility and sustainability work.

He has worked in Europe, the US and over 30 emerging markets of Africa, Asia and Latin America. He has advised a wide range of international companies in industries as diverse as food and drinks, mobile phones, oil and pharmaceuticals.

In the 1970s, David worked for the British Trades Union Congress and in the 1980s he joined Levi Strauss & Co in Europe, then moved to San Francisco, where he worked for the company's Ethics and Social Responsibility Committee. He returned to the UK in the early 1990s to set up his business.

He is a graduate of the University of London, with a master's degree in philosophy and education. He is a member of the board of the Institute of Corporate Responsibility and Sustainability and an associate of the Centre for Sustainable Business Practices at the University of Northampton.